How to Choos

Advisors:

Getting the Best Professional Family Business Advice

Craig E. Aronoff, Ph.D. and
John L. Ward, Ph.D.

Family Business Leadership Series, No. 6

Family Enterprise Publishers
P.O. Box 4356
Marietta, GA 30061-4356
800-551-0633
www.efamilybusiness.com

ISSN: 1071-5010
ISBN: 0-9651011-6-9

Fourth Printing

Family Business Leadership Series

We believe that family businesses are special, not only to the families that own and manage them but to our society and to the private enterprise system. Having worked and interacted with hundreds of family enterprises in the past twenty years, we offer the insights of that experience and the collected wisdom of the world's best and most successful family firms.

This volume is a part of a series offering practical guidance for family businesses seeking to manage the special challenges and opportunities confronting them.

To order additional copies, contact:
Family Enterprise Publishers[SM]
1220-B Kennestone Circle
Post Office Box 4356
Marietta, Georgia 30061-4356
Tel: 800-551-0633
Web Sites: www.efamilybusiness.com

Quantity discounts are available.

Other volumes in the series include:

Family Business Succession: The Final Test of Greatness

Family Meetings: How to Build a Stronger Family and a Stronger Business

Another Kind of Hero: Preparing Successors For Leadership

How Families Work Together

Family Business Compensation

Financing Transitions: Managing Capital and Liquidity in the Family Business

Family Business Governance: Maximizing Family and Business Potential

Preparing Your Family Business For Strategic Change

Making Sibling Teams Work: The Next Generation

Developing Family Business Policies: Your Guide to the Future

Family Business Values: How To Assure A Legacy of Continuity and Success

More Than Family: Non-Family Executives in the Family Business

Make Change Your Family Business Tradition

Family Business Ownership: How To Be An Effective Shareholder

Contents

Preface vii

I. **The Value of Good Advice** 1

II. **Why So Few Business Owners Get and Accept Good Advice** 9

III. **Benchmarks in Advisory Service: What Is the Best You Can Expect?** 15

IV. **Red Flags: Warning Signals in Advisory Relationships** 31

V. **Finding and Choosing an Advisor** 39

VI. **Managing and Evaluating Advisors** 45

VII. **Summary** 55

Appendix 57

Index 63

Tables and Exhibits

Table 1:
What to Expect from Advisors 2

Table 2:
Using Advisors as the Family Business Matures 5

Table 3:
Use of Advisors by Family Businesses 11

Table 4:
Marks of Excellence in Advisors 16

Table 5:
Recognizing Family Business Professionals 19

Table 6:
The Special Needs of Family Businesses 26

Table 7:
Red Flags in Client-Advisor Relationships 32

Table 8:
A 12-Point Checklist for Selecting
Professional Advisors 41

Exhibit 1:
The Spectrum of Advisory Quality 22

Exhibit 2:
The Competing Capital Demands on Family Business 25

Exhibit 3:
Advice from the Pros 42

Preface

The success and survival of your family business may depend on the professionals you choose to advise you on matters of finance, law, taxes, family relations, business strategy, succession and other issues. The good news is that never before have so many experts been competing to serve family businesses.

And never before have they had so much to offer.

Recognizing the economic importance of family business, hundreds of professional advisors are building expertise in the unique strengths and needs of family-owned firms. And in a major step forward for family business, a growing number of these professionals are using proactive skills to help business owners plan for the future health and family ownership of the business.

How can a business owner best tap this resource? And what quality of service should he or she expect?

This booklet offers guidance on when to consult an advisor and what you have a right to expect when you do. It offers practical tips for finding and selecting advisors who will respect your goals, values and objectives, and for managing them efficiently once you do. It sets benchmarks for excellent practices among professional family business advisors and alerts the reader to warning signals in advisory relationships.

"A family business is such a treasure to its owners. They want it to be handled very carefully. They must have confidence that an advisor is capable of doing that," says Leonard Bock, president of Bock, Benjamin & Co., an investment banking concern. "Every skill and every experience that I've ever had over a lifetime has come into play in helping family businesses. It's a constantly challenging situation," he says.

Our focus is exclusively advisors to the family business. This booklet does not deal with professionals who specialize primarily in family issues, like family therapists or psychoanalysts. Nor does it discuss such general business advisors as marketing consultants or systems analysts.

Instead, by drawing on our own extensive family business consulting experience and the expertise of 16 top family business experts in a multidisciplinary range of professional fields, this book describes the special qualities of outstanding family business advisors and prepares the business owner to draw on their skills. Each contributor is identified in the manuscript, and a guide to contributors with additional information on each is in the Appendix. These experts are professionals with outstanding reputations, with whom we have personal experience. They represent the full range of professional disciplines a family business owner might typically need, and they are geographically representative of many areas of the country. All have consciously thought, spoken and taught others about what constitutes excellence in serving family businesses. Their contribution has been invaluable to our effort.

Craig E. Aronoff, Ph.D.

John L. Ward, Ph.D.

I. The Value of Good Advice: *When Do Most Business Owners Need Help?*

■

"No man is wise enough by himself."

— Titus Maccius Plautus, 254-184 BC

■

Leading a family business can be one of the most complex jobs imaginable.

For its owner, the family business is a crucible for some of life's great challenges: growing a company, leading a family, nurturing loved ones — the same crucible in which the business owner's own life story and personal financial security are formed.

Every business owner needs help from time to time. Good advisors can assist by drawing on their experience with many family businesses. They can help solve problems and resolve conflicts. They can ease the isolation of running a business by showing that other business owners share similar problems. In that process, the advisor also protects business owners from the need to re-invent the wheel.

Yet many business owners don't get the advice they need and deserve. Many hesitate to seek the best advisors. Instead, they "underhire" out of modesty, loyalty to longtime advisors they have outgrown, or a sense of comfort with advisors who don't challenge them. Other business owners aren't sure when to call an advisor or what kind is best suited to help. Table 1 summarizes the services provided by various kinds of family business professionals. Table 2 shows what advisors can be most helpful as the family business passes through three common stages:

- A first-generation or entrepreneurial phase, when the business is usually owned and led by one person, typically the founder;
- A second-generation or "family partnership" stage, when the business is managed by a few controlling owners who are usually siblings;
- A third-generation or "family dynasty" stage when the shareholder base broadens to include cousins with family members both active and inactive in the business.

TABLE 1

WHAT TO EXPECT FROM ADVISORS

Accountant. Tax planning and preparation of returns. Organizing and interpreting financial statements. Improving financial management and reporting, sometimes by helping design new systems. Helping with business transfer, succession, estate and family compensation planning. Providing informal financial and management advice and mentoring successors. General business advice.

Attorney. Helping negotiate contracts and other documents such as stock restriction and buy-sell agreements. Helping determine the form of business ownership and capital structure. Attending board meetings at the chairman's discretion and reviewing board-level transactions. Acting as a diplomatic "go-between" for a business owner and a mentor for successors. Resolving disputes through compromise or litigation. Preparing estate plans, wills and trust documents and reviewing them every one to five years. Helping plan for payment of estate tax obligations or financing shareholder buyouts. Preparing prenuptial agreements and providing counsel regarding plans to bring new family members into the business. Helping establish business governance policies to enhance the likelihood of successful transfer of the business to younger generations — especially by helping set up an effective board of directors and policies for employment and promotion of family members.

Banker. Making loans and setting up lines of credit. Helping with pensions and 401K plans. Helping decide how to finance growth, succession or shareholder demands for liquidity. Helping evaluate debt-equity ratios. Raising timely questions about succession and estate planning. Informally, instructing successors in financial skills.

Executive search consultant. Identifying and recruiting key non-family managers and directors, including "bridge" managers between generations of family management. Helping reenergize the stagnant organization or professionalize management through key hires. Helping identify and fill gaps in management.

Family business consultant. Encouraging development and implementation of succession, estate, strategic and personal financial plans. Helping develop successors. Helping plan family compensation and entry of new family members into the business. Helping plan shareholder liquidity or buyout programs. Helping revitalize the business. Setting up active outside boards. Fostering family unity and communication, organizing family meetings and developing family statements of mission or purpose. Generally, helping family businesses through transitions and helping perpetuate family ownership.

TABLE 1 *(continued)*

WHAT TO EXPECT FROM ADVISORS

Financial advisor. Helping business owners identify and choose among various ways of addressing the liquidity needs of shareholders or the capital needs of the business. Anticipating capital and liquidity needs. Assisting in implementing capital or liquidity programs. Restructuring ownership to perpetuate family control or concentrate ownership in certain segments of the shareholder base. Informally, helping educate successors about financial management. (Many financial advisors also provide the investment banking services described below.)

Insurance agent. Alerting the business owner to the need for insurance to protect against large, unpredictable demands for cash in the future. Specifically, helping select policies to pay estate taxes, finance shareholder buyouts, ensure survivors' financial security, incentivize key non-family executives, repay debt or guard against the disability or loss of a key manager. Acting as a catalyst for estate planning. Educating the business owner about complex insurance alternatives, policy illustrations and the differences among various policies and insurers. Providing annuities or life insurance to reward key employees.

Investment banker. Valuing assets and businesses. Identifying prospective buyers or sellers of assets or businesses and helping manage sales and acquisitions. Identifying potential investors and making public or private placements of stock or debt. Helping assess debt-equity ratios and dividend policy. Designing shareholder redemption programs.

Organizational development specialist. Helping build teamwork, cohesiveness, communication and a sense of purpose within a business. Helping with successor development and selection, team-building or team transition among siblings or cousins. Designing career paths, compensation plans and performance-appraisal systems for family and non-family managers. Helping revitalize stagnant organizations and professionalize management.

Psychologist. Diagnosing and helping heal psychological tensions, morale issues and relationship problems in a business. Helping family members in transition. Helping resolve conflicts and build cohesiveness among family members. Helping business leaders make the transition to retirement. Helping successors develop their own identity. Improving family communication. Evaluating key managers. Resolving issues raised by bringing in key non-family managers.

(table continued on following page)

TABLE 1 *(continued)*

What to Expect From Advisors

Trust officer. Administering trusts and managing trust assets in beneficiaries' best interest. Increasingly, counselling business owners informally and providing referrals to experts on valuation, estate planning, estate and gift tax planning, investment management and other services. If a business is controlled by a trust, reviewing business performance, helping identify candidates to fill management gaps and serving as a director if needed.

Valuation expert. Valuing a business based on its management, assets, performance, outlook and research into comparable companies with established market values. Using this information to help value estates, gifts of stock, divorce and litigation settlements, shareholder liquidity programs, fairness opinions, ESOPs or executive stock plans. Helping plan transfer of ownership and management of estate taxes.

TABLE 2

USING ADVISORS AS THE FAMILY BUSINESS MATURES*

	STAGE 1: Owner-Operated "Entrepreneurial Succession" Stage	STAGE 2: Second Generation "Family Partnership" Stage	STAGE 3: Third Generation and Beyond: The "Family Dynasty" Stage
Accountant	• Developing financial controls and systems ➧ • Helping develop banking relationship • Estate and ownership succession planning ➧ • Succession planning ➧ • Mentoring successors ➧ • Transfer to next generation ➧	• Reviewing financial reporting and management ➧ • Tax consequences of various ownership structures ➧ • Bonus and incentive plans for managers ➧ • Coordinating family members' estate plans ➧ • Advice on business expansion and growth ➧ • Reviewing banking relationships ➧	• Estate master plans to perpetuate the business
Lawyer	• Incorporating • Helping develop banking relationship • Estate planning ➧ • Succession planning ➧ • Mentoring successors ➧ • Setting up active outside board ➧	• Developing buy-sell agreements among siblings • Coordinating family members' estate plans ➧ • Prenuptial agreements for siblings • Structuring ownership ➧ • Compensating key nonfamily managers ➧ • Helping plan for family members' entry into business ➧	• Estate master plans to perpetuate the business
Banker	• Making operating loans ➧ • Financing growth • Improving financial reporting • Mentoring successors ➧	• Planning to provide liquidity to family members ➧ • Advice on business expansion and growth ➧ • Financing business expansion and growth ➧	• Planning allocation of capital

*Certain basic advisory roles are omitted, such as an accountant's preparations of tax returns. ➧ indicates a continuing function through the life of the family business.

TABLE 2 *(continued)*

	STAGE 1: Owner-Operated "Entrepreneurial Succession" Stage	**STAGE 2: Second Generation "Family Partnership" Stage**	**STAGE 3: Third Generation and Beyond: The "Family Dynasty" Stage**
Insurance Advisor	• Life insurance for financial security ➧ • Life insurance for estate taxes ➧ • Insuring and rewarding key employees ➧ • Acting as catalyst for estate planning ➧	• Financing stock buybacks ➧ • Financing family security ➧	
Valuation Consultant	• Estate planning ➧ • Valuing gifts of stock ➧	• Planning to provide shareholder liquidity ➧ • Structuring shareholder buyouts or loans ➧	• Valuing stock for executive stock plans, ESOPs
Psychologist	• Helping the founder "let go" • Helping the successor establish identity • Career paths for second generation • Building family communication skills ➧	• Evaluating key people ➧ • Building sibling teamwork and communication ➧ • Professionalizing management ➧ • Resolving family conflict ➧	• Educating family on consequences of wealth • Articulating family values, history and culture • Building shareholder harmony and commitment • Assessing family member strength and weaknesses
Organization Development Specialist	• Intergenerational business planning ➧ • Succession planning ➧ • Career paths for second generation • Building skills and teamwork among siblings ➧	• Revitalizing strategy • Planning family and nonfamily compensation ➧ • Formalizing management • Career paths for nonfamily managers	• Counseling family members for career development • Building shareholder harmony and commitment • Family conflict resolution • Professionalizing management
Search Consultant	• Recruiting nonfamily interim managers ➧ • Recruiting outside directors ➧	• Revitalizing the organization through new hires ➧ • Filling gaps in newly professionalized management	• Building depth and breadth of management • Helping identify management personnel needs

*Certain basic advisory roles are omitted, such as an accountant's preparations of tax returns. ➧ indicates a continuing function through the life of the family business.

TABLE 2 *(continued)*

	STAGE 1: Owner-Operated "Entrepreneurial Succession" Stage	STAGE 2: Second Generation "Family Partnership" Stage	STAGE 3: Third Generation and Beyond: The "Family Dynasty" Stage
Family Business Consultant	• Management succession planning ➧ • Ownership succession planning ➧ • Entry of family members into the business • Beginning family meetings • Setting up active outside board • Mentoring successors ➧	• Planning compensation for family members ➧ • Pay and incentives for key nonfamily employees ➧ • Family code of conduct • Developing shareholder liquidity programs • Planning in-laws' role • Revitalizing strategy • Involving talented third generation family members • Career paths for family and nonfamily managers ➧ • Planning to perpetuate family leadership ➧	• Shareholder harmony, commitment and education • Family conflict resolution • Planning allocation of capital • Structuring a portfolio of businesses • Developing a family council or organization • Developing a family mission statement • Planning a role of inactive shareholders • Planning ownership structure • Planning family linkage with the business • Articulating family tradition, history, culture
Financial Advisor	• Planning ways to finance growth ➧ • Developing financial reporting and management • Mentoring successors ➧ • Helping structure ownership transition ➧	• Planning to provide shareholder liquidity ➧ • Advice on business expansion and growth ➧ • Anticipating capital needs ➧ • Financing shareholder buyouts or liquidity programs ➧	• Reviewing ownership structure • Financing business expansion and growth • Planning allocation of capital
Trust Officer	• Estate planning ➧ • Gifting of stock ➧ • Planning trusts ➧	• Planning ownership structure ➧	

*Certain basic advisory roles are omitted, such as an accountant's preparations of tax returns. ➧ indicates a continuing function through the life of the family business.

II. *Why So Few Business Owners Get and Accept Good Advice*

■

"Advice is seldom welcome; and those who want it the most always like it the least."

— Philip Dormer Stanhope, Earl of Chesterfield

■

Few business owners use professional advisors wisely. Nearly one-third of family businesses have no trusted advisor outside the family, a recent survey by Massachusetts Mutual Life Insurance Co. shows. (Please see Table 3.)

Let's take a look at ten common attitudes that keep business owners from getting the advice they need:

***1. "I can solve the problem myself."* Many business owners are used to being in charge and having people look to them for answers. This pattern can be habit-forming, leading the business owner to feel he or she should have all the answers.**

While self-reliance is a virtue that has built some great businesses, it also can be an obstacle to solving complex family business problems efficiently. An advisor with experience in many businesses can protect a business owner from reinventing the wheel. He or she also can keep problems from mushrooming into crises.

2. "I don't want anyone throwing up roadblocks to my plans." Business owners are action-oriented doers and may not even think of calling an advisor until they have committed to a course of action. This tendency builds on itself. The more decisions a business owner has made before seeking advice, the more likely he or she is to be embarrassed by an advisor's reaction.

But however uncomfortable it may be to admit to people who admire you that you need to change your plans, it is sometimes necessary to avert bigger problems. As tensions rose within the Bingham family of *Louisville Courier-Journal* fame, Management Planning Inc., a financial appraisal concern, advised the family leader, Barry Bingham Sr., to set aside his carefully laid estate plans long enough to buy out Sally Bingham, the family's chief dissenter, at the stock's publicly traded value.

Removing her from the trust might ease family tensions, even though it meant a one-time transaction at a price higher than the one already established, suggested a Management Planning advisor. But Mr. Bingham refused that counsel in fear of disrupting his estate plan, insisting, "I'm not buying her out at a penny more." What followed, as history shows, was an upheaval, led by Sally Bingham, that was far more destructive than any change in an estate plan might have been.

3. "Professional advisors should be used only as a last resort." This attitude, a corollary to No. 2, casts professional advisors as firefighters — a necessary evil or defensive weapon to avoid lawsuits, IRS audits or other calamities.

It usually means business owners call advisors too late — "when the canoe is over the waterfall," says Henry C. Krasnow, a partner in Krasnow Sanberg & Cohen, a law firm. If a crisis erupts over succession, shareholder discord or other unaddressed fundamentals, the business owner and advisor then face the impossible task of "paddling back upstream over the falls," he says. Calling an advisor early can help the owner learn where the edge of the waterfall is and avoid it, Mr. Krasnow says.

4. "An outsider could never understand my business." Some business owners believe "an advisor is someone who borrows your watch to tell you what time it is." They contend, "By the time I invest enough so that an advisor can understand my situation, I could have solved it myself."

This rationale is a handy excuse to keep the family business a closed system. All businesses are unique, but all share some characteristics as well. Otherwise there would be no business schools, no movement of executives between businesses, no useful books on business. If an advisor is well chosen, as discussed later in this booklet, he or she will bring relevant experience to your business and will probably be a surprisingly quick study as well.

5. "High-powered experts wouldn't be interested in my business." Even successful entrepreneurs often are too humble, unassuming or unsure of themselves to seek out the best advisors. Despite their success, these business owners often hesitate to apply to professional advisors the same high performance standards they impose on themselves and their employees.

This tendency begins early, often with a reluctance as a startup to seek out a commercial lender, says Linda Tubbs, a senior vice president and a

TABLE 3

USE OF ADVISORS BY FAMILY BUSINESSES

Selected Advisors From Outside the Family Rated "Most Important" by Family Business Owners

Advisor	Percent
No one	30%
Family members not in the business	2%
Friends	3%
Business peers	3%
Banker	4%
Managers in company	4%
Attorneys	9%
Accountants	31%

SOURCE: Survey of 614 family business owners by Massachusetts Mutual Life Insurance Co., Springfield, Mass., September, 1993.

commercial banking manager for First Interstate Bank of Oregon. Many business owners don't realize that advisors usually like to see prospective clients at any stage. "The process (of applying) could provide them with some free counseling," Ms. Tubbs says.

As the business grows, many owners tend to stick with longtime advisors whom they may have outgrown. But just as a business owner would not settle for a supplier who failed to meet his or her needs, he or she should not settle for an advisor who is less than challenging. No matter how formidable their expertise may seem at first, top-flight family business advisors should be approachable and communicative, and should provide helpful referrals if they are unable to help a client themselves. If business owners demanded as much from their professional advisors as they do from their employees and themselves, running their businesses would likely be easier, more profitable and less lonely.

6. "An advisor will raise a lot of issues I don't have time to bother with right now." Many business owners fear that confiding in an advisor will open a Pandora's box. Some believe advisors will raise questions they can't answer or that threaten their personal confidence or control. Others sense that an advisor's probing may thrust them into "the planning triangle" — the web of financial, estate, succession and family issues that must be addressed for a family business to thrive through generations. Indeed, a good advisor often must understand a business owner's goals in all these areas to help solve problems in any one of them. The business owner may not want to take that leap, preferring to keep everything quiet.

Left unchecked, problems can worsen until a client reaches "a point of enormous pain," says Kathy Wiseman of Working Systems, a consultant specializing in family and organizational development. In families, adds Harry Levinson of The Levinson Institute, a psychologist, consultant and noted author on succession and other management issues, the desire to preserve peace often leads to "perennial conflict and lack of resolution." Only by addressing issues head-on can these unhealthy symptoms be healed.

7. "I don't want to share any information with an outsider." Many business owners place such a high value on secrecy that they refuse to share any information with non-family people. In fact, confidentiality is a baseline requirement of professional advisors. The smallest doubt about an advisor's ability to respect business and family secrets is enough to disqualify that person.

This argument, a corollary to No. 4, also misses the potential value to any business of using a "sounding board," an informed person with a fresh perspective and an ability to respond objectively. This can be crucial in helping the family business avoid growing stale or out of touch. One entrepreneur was mystified by the results of an employee survey. For years, the man had heard praise for his business as "a nice place to work," with generous salaries, perks and paternalistic benefits. But now, surveyed employees were calling him authoritarian and overcontrolling. "He simply couldn't understand why on the one hand they were so appreciative, and on the other so critical," Dr. Levinson says. The advisor's role, he says, "was to help him understand that the world had changed, that people had different expectations than when he got started" — including a desire for more participation in decisionmaking.

8. "Professional advisors cost too much." Nowhere is it more likely true that "you get what you pay for" than with professional advisors. Yet many business owners assume all advisors are overpriced. Many also fear they lack control over fees. In fact, advisory relationships can be managed for cost-effectiveness, as discussed later in this booklet.

And many business owners undervalue the financial importance of sound decisionmaking. "To focus solely on (the) cost (of an advisor) is doing yourself a disservice," says Ross Nager, national director, family wealth planning, for Arthur Andersen & Co., a large accounting and management consulting firm. **"The real cost of advice is not what you pay for it. It is either the cost that you incur when you take the advice and find out that it's wrong — which obviously can devastate the business. Or it's the opportunity cost of receiving the advice but not taking it because you don't trust your advisor."**

Adds Michael Horvitz, a partner with Jones, Day, Reavis & Pogue, a major law firm, and director of privately owned business for the firm's tax group: "Any lawyer or advisor who really provides good service will over time pay for himself or herself."

9. "Our longtime attorney (or accountant or banker) is a family friend and knows us best. We don't need anyone else." **Many business owners operate in closed systems with little affirmation except growth in sales or the loyalty of key employees.** They may place such a premium on loyalty that they rely on old friends for advice, even after the business outgrows the friend's expertise.

Other business owners risk becoming too dependent on the advice of a single person. For instance, an owner may ask a longtime family attorney to prepare a will and trust documents, rather than consulting an estate planner, says John Patterson, senior vice president, NationsBank Corp., a major bank holding company. While the documents may be excellent, the underlying planning may miss many of the complexities of passing on a family business, exposing the business and the family to major financial damage.

At the extreme, families may rely on a loyal advisor as a manager of last resort. That can be tragic; while advisors may know a lot about your business, they rarely know anything about running your business.

10. "I'm unsure of how relationships with professional advisors work." The idea of calling a professional advisor sometimes raises so many questions for business owners that they avoid it. How could an advisor help? What will he or she expect of me? How will I explain it to the family? What information will I have to disclose? Will he or she press for solutions that don't fit our business? How can an outsider understand our situation?

This booklet strives to answer those questions and more, empowering business owners to make the best choices for their businesses and their families.

III. Benchmarks in Advisory Service
What Is the Best You Can Expect?

■

benchmark: something that serves as a standard by which others may be measured.

— Webster's dictionary

■

Good advisors to the family business are more than just experts in their field.

Outstanding family business professionals demonstrate a second level of skills, many of them unique to serving family business. Good advisors understand the business and the family. They have in-depth knowledge of the transitions all family businesses go through. They have strong interpersonal skills and are capable of working with all family members. In many situations, they are able to strengthen not only the business, but the family. (Please see Table 4.)

Let's take a closer look at these benchmarks.

1. Maintains up-to-date technical knowledge and shows strong interest in and commitment to his or her field. Technical expertise and the discipline and drive to stay abreast of new developments are essential to the excellent family business advisor. The advisor should be so well plugged in that he or she can routinely advise the business owner of new developments that affect the business. An increasing number of family business advisors are cross-trained in more than one discipline. Others have a network of other professionals they rely on for breadth of knowledge. "It's a pretty complicated world. You need an advisor or group of advisors who have a broad wing span," Michael Horvitz says.

Your advisor's technical knowledge should suit firms of your size and ownership structure. A valuation professional, for instance, should have experience valuing family businesses in your industry, says Management Planning, Inc.'s Jim Roberts. Relying on advisors who only know other markets can be costly. Leonard Bock tells of valuing one business, a partnership with uneven profitability, and receiving an offer for the firm that was within 10 percent of his valuation. The controlling partner then sought and received a valuation twice that high from a Wall Street investment banking firm that was accustomed to dealing with larger,

TABLE 4

BENCHMARKS OF EXCELLENCE IN ADVISORS

1. Maintains up-to-date technical knowledge and shows strong interest in and commitment to his or her field
2. Communicates openly in clear, simple language, helping educate family members when appropriate
3. Seeks to know the family and business in depth
4. Understands how families work and how the family and the business relate to each other
5. Gives advice and counsel that suit both the family and the business
6. Initiates periodic meetings with the client for update and review
7. Is resourceful on clients' behalf, spotting opportunities and sharing information and contacts
8. Shows empathy, patience and trustworthiness
9. Is willing to work with successor generations
10. Raises questions about the future
11. Promotes collaboration among advisors
12. Gives honest advice, even when it may jeopardize the client relationship

publicly traded clients. On that basis, the partner rejected the offer. Within six months, the business lost a client that accounted for twenty percent of its sales. Under pressure from lenders, the partner was forced to sell for far less than the offer Mr. Bock had secured. "The owner got advice from a reputable source, but the source's reputation and experience was from a world completely different from his," Mr. Bock says.

The good advisor also displays the enthusiasm that comes from really liking one's specialty and enjoying the work. Without prompting, he or she thinks about the client frequently and generates new ideas and insights.

2. Communicates frequently and openly in clear, simple language. A good advisor should be willing and able to explain issues in clear, simple language. "You get paid for your ability to take knowledge and simplify it to the point where it is understandable" to clients, says Joseph Blum of J.F. Blum & Associates, a senior Massachusetts Mutual Life Insurance Co. agent who specializes in succession and estate-planning issues. That often means "you must understand family issues as well as tax issues at the most complex level imaginable."

For example, a life insurance consultant should be able to explain to a business owner why competing companies' premiums on a $1 million life insurance policy differ so widely, how rates are set and why some policies are riskier than others. Mr. Blum once set a meeting with a bank chairman whose estate was valued at $17 million simply to explain why premiums for various policies weren't comparable. When he was finished, the banker "looked at me and said, 'This is the first time in my life I have understood where these numbers come from.' He was 72 years old and dealing with a senior partner at a Big Six accounting firm, and no one had ever slowed down long enough to explain it to him," Mr. Blum says. "If you can explain such things in simple language, you're doing a great service. Once the business owner has the tools, he can do his own analysis."

3. Seeks to know the family and the business in depth. A good advisor goes well beyond responding to client questions or requests for meetings. He or she works to understand the family and the business in depth. The advisor reads up on the company and the family, looking at meeting minutes, catalogs, brochures and histories when appropriate. He or she volunteers for plant or office visits to see how the business is doing and meet managers or employees. The good advisor learns about family members' interests and circumstances, volunteering to call or meet with them when appropriate. And he or she occasionally will attend business or family events such as a business anniversary or a family ceremony.

All of these activities help an advisor gain a deeper understanding of the family's history and values and the culture of the business — factors that can help in offering advice and counsel that is on target for the particular needs of each client.

4. Understands how families work and how the family and business relate to each other. The complex and unique dynamics of a family can foil the best technical solution an advisor might offer. "Anyone who thinks that he can achieve the best interests of the business but remain oblivious to the best interests of the family is going to encounter problems," says Michael L. Fay, a senior partner at Hale and Dorr, a major Boston law firm.

Irving L. Blackman, founding partner of Blackman Kallick Bartelstein, a Chicago accounting firm, adds, "If your advisor doesn't explore, understand and deal effectively with human elements (of issues), even the most brilliant, money-saving technical plan will fail. Or the plan will never be signed, completed or fully implemented."

As discussed in *How Families Work Together*, No. 4 in the **Family Business Leadership Series**, families share a multi-generational history of ancestors, events and relationships. That history is filled with behavioral patterns that influence the present and the future. Any time a business family reaches a point of stress or transition, these patterns can surface in forceful and sometimes puzzling ways.

Any professional who advises a business family in depth needs a healthy respect for the power of family history. The advisor should take time to develop a "cultural appreciation" for the family business, including its history and values and the language of the entrepreneur and family, Dr. Levinson says. "One has to be something of an anthropologist," he says.

As discussed later, a business owner can identify an advisor well-grounded in the workings of families in several ways. (Please see Table 5.) One indicator is the questions the advisor asks. François M. de Visscher of de Visscher & Co., a financial-advisory and investment banking concern, "spends a considerable amount of time obtaining an understanding of the family. That goes from understanding the history of the family and how the business was started, to who got involved, what branches are more active now and the objectives of current shareholders," he says. "We spend an equal amount of time assimilating the growth potential, capital needs and value-creation potential of the business. On the basis of those two big blocks of information, on the business side and the family side, we develop the solutions. Every client is different and every set of solutions we propose is different."

In preparation for initial client meetings, Mr. Blackman asks clients not only for financial statements, tax returns, wills and trusts, but for a copy of the family tree. In the meeting, he asks "open-ended questions in a friendly, nonthreatening manner," he says. He also spends as much time as necessary with a client, listening carefully and "mirroring back" his or her objectives, concerns and fears to make sure they are understood.

Mr. Fay identifies several criteria an attorney to a family business should be able to satisfy, including: Have family needs been identified and distinguished from business needs? Does the lawyer understand the

TABLE 5

RECOGNIZING FAMILY-BUSINESS PROFESSIONALS

1. Do they have experience working with family businesses?
2. Are they abreast of literature on serving the family business? Do they subscribe to respected publications in the field?
3. Are they respected by other family business professionals? Have they written or spoken publicly on serving family business?
4. Can they provide references from successful family businesses?
5. Do they network among other family business advisors? Do they attend family business conferences?
6. Are they familiar with the dynamics of families — known among professionals as "family systems theory?"
7. Do they show interest and concern for family factors as they affect your business?

family system? In particular, how do family relationships affect the business? Do family conflicts impede business planning? Can the lawyer suggest improvements in the governance of the business to help resolve such conflicts? Does the lawyer recognize which family business problems are not legal problems? Does the lawyer appreciate how much his or her own personal experience affects his or her perception of family issues?

Hale and Dorr takes the unusual step of training partners and associates in the complexities of family business. "I've never seen so many young lawyers whose jaws went thud on the table" as when senior partners debated complex family business case studies, Mr. Fay says. The fact that reasonable technical solutions can have completely different ramifications for a business-owning family is "an eye-opener" even for the partners, he says.

5. Gives advice and counsel that work for both the family and the business. The best advisors put their understanding of family business to work by meeting the family business owner where he or she lives: amid a jungle of powerful and often conflicting demands. Here are some examples.

Nontechnical solutions. Good advisors see family business issues neither in technical terms nor in terms of family dynamics, but in both contexts at once.

A great advisor must be able to help the business owner address family issues — not avoid them. If a business owner says, "I want to gift stock to my children, but I'm worried about the spouses," some advisors will steer the conversation away: "Gosh, that's really unfortunate. Did you know Congress is doing thus-and-so?" Others might offer a technical solution — "Yeah, you need an XYZ trust to keep your stock out of divorce court!" While the advisor may expertly produce the necessary paperwork, it does nothing to solve the more complex underlying problem or equip the family to work together in the future, Ross Nager says.

The best solutions combine in-depth technical knowledge with sensitivity to the ongoing needs of the family. Compensation planning in the family business, for instance, is "not just a matter of going out to find what a similar person in a public company makes. It's knowing how to structure compensation specifically to reduce or avoid the family feuding that can go on around this issue," Mr. Nager says.

Such solutions often result in policies that not only resolve immediate issues, but transfer to other kinds of problems. If the business owner is worried about in-laws' owning stock, for instance, an advisor might not only help with a solution, but help work on an overarching policy on family participation in the business that would prevent future conflict.

No Formulas. From an outsider's perspective, solutions to some family business problems may seem obvious. But advisors offering pat formulas for family business problems are usually about as helpful as backseat drivers or Monday morning quarterbacks.

Solutions must be designed with the unique characteristics and potential of each family in mind. Rather than suggesting a standard buy-sell agreement for every family partnership, for instance, an advisor should take time to understand the goals and capabilities of all the family members involved and their potential over the years. Two brothers who were partners in a family business approached a family-business consultant for advice on whether their buy-sell agreement should be updated.

"Let me guess the provisions," the consultant said. "As soon as one of you dies, the other is required to buy out his entire ownership position. But what happens if your children have grown up and hold substantial management positions in the business? And the son of the one who dies is the successor? And the surviving brother buys out the entire ownership position, and the successor is left with no ownership? Is that what you want to happen?" the consultant asked.

"How did you know what was in our buy-sell agreement?" the brothers asked, astonished.

"Find yourselves a lawyer who will ask some of the questions I just asked," the consultant said.

A good advisor is able to set aside all assumptions and meet the business family where it is. One third-generation business owner was excited about bringing his two sons into the business. But while his third and oldest child, a daughter, had gotten an MBA and was enthused about working in the business, he had difficulty working with her. Though talented and smart, she couldn't keep deadlines or other business disciplines. Though the business owner felt his differences with his daughter were irreconcilable, he did not want to be seen as chauvinistic.

Rather than pressing for a politically correct solution, his advisor, Ms. Wiseman, helped him see that his problems with his daughter were rooted in a family process in which he played a part. In the past, women in the family had never been given the opportunity to participate in the business, though their husbands had always been given positions and treated equally. With all the best intentions, this business owner was trying to shatter those entrenched patterns of behavior. Yet in the case of his daughter, just wanting to act in a nonchauvinistic way was not enough.

Ms. Wiseman helped the business owner examine reasons for failure of the arrangement, then helped him as he thought through the process of choosing among alternative solutions, communicating and executing his decision — and managing the repercussions. Ultimately, the father reached his goal of equitable and respectful treatment for his daughter, but by following a different path: The sons bought her out at a premium and the father helped her set up her own business.

A good advisor, Ms. Wiseman says, "allows the family to be the best they can be, and the business to be the best it can be, regardless of what the consultant thinks is best."

Insight on many levels. Just as a builder reinforces a house on many levels, a good advisor goes beyond the problem posed to help the business owner at many levels. (Please see Exhibit 1.)

The potential for painful conflict loomed large as one second-generation family business plunged into succession planning. The CEO's son

EXHIBIT 1

The Spectrum of Advisory Quality

Great advisors go beyond answering technical questions to help on a spectrum ranging from solid basic technical advice to the most skilled, in-depth and caring professional support.

FUNDAMENTAL EXPERTISE

- Possesses necessary technical expertise
- Stays abreast of new developments
- Proactive; suggests solutions
- Contacts you for an update
- Asks for meetings solely for an update
- Promotes collaboration among advisors
- Evokes trust in discussing sensitive family issues
- Listens patiently to sensitive family issues
- Has compassion for the business owner
- Helps find appropriate nontechnical solutions
- Brings to table broader skills than you expected or asked
- Has courage to stand by convictions

HIGHLY SKILLED AND CARING SUPPORT

SOURCE: Ross Nager, Arthur Andersen & Co.

was a candidate for leadership, as were the son of the CEO's older brother and several non-family managers. Inactive shareholders were anxious about the choice because they depended on income from the business and wanted the next generation of managers to sustain its performance.

Seeing that the questions raised went far beyond the capabilities of inside successor candidates, Dr. Levinson, the advisor, met the issue on several levels. First, "it was the better part of wisdom to interview inactive shareholders and get some sense of who they were and what they felt about the business, its leadership, the son and the others in the organization," he says. "They could well have upset the apple cart on any choice that had been made, and voted their shares in a way that could have been destructive."

Second, Dr. Levinson helped evaluate the business skills of the inside successor candidates and identify five contenders, including one of the sons. All needed seasoning and training that would take at least five years. "That meant somebody else had to be brought in from the outside, which was difficult to swallow for the CEO, the family members and even the people who had to wait their turn in the CEO role," Dr. Levinson says.

Third, he helped everyone involved understand, in the process of interviewing them, the need for continuing strong management, laying the groundwork for a non-family "bridge" manager to sustain the business.

Finally, he also helped avert future problems by interviewing outside candidates for the CEO's job, helping them understand the family situation and "appreciate what they would be getting into," he says.

Opening doors to planning. An effective advisor often uses immediate problems as a catalyst for needed future planning.

One business owner hired an advisor to help decide whether his two sons were ready to take over the business. The sons had worked mostly for their father on special projects. After interviewing key employees, outside consultants and directors, the advisor concluded that the sons had the ability to lead the business but needed broader experience. The successors needed to work with key managers in the business and earn their respect. Also, when asked in interviews who came up with important new strategic ideas and decisions, managers pointed to the business owner.

"Could you do it if the owner were not around?" the advisor asked.

The managers thought they probably could, but said they had not needed to generate new ideas and lacked any experience doing it.

The advisor realized that the founder had successfully mapped the business' strategy through intuition and instinct. But so far, he had done it alone, leaving the business lacking bench strength and his sons without needed management experience.

The advisor returned to the business owner with two recommendations: First, the business' key managers need experience working with your sons, he said. Give the successors a meaningful project you believe they can do well, and let them work together on it with key managers.

Second, the managers need experience in envisioning the future of the business, he told the owner. The advisor recommended a strategic planning project that would involve key managers, helping them understand the company's markets and envision the future. "If your business is going to succeed into the next generation, the business has to be successful in its own right," the advisor said — not as an extension of the founder.

The advisor stuck around to help implement the recommendations. As a result of the strategic planning effort, the company took some steps that increased sales, says Mr. Nager, the advisor on the case. And the sons' continuing work with key managers has earned their respect.

This solution accomplished more than the business owner had asked. First, it gave successors and key managers experience working together on a trial basis with support from the advisor, helping them develop needed skills and trust. Second, by stressing the sons' and key managers' need to learn to envision the future, the advisor was able to help the business owner begin much-needed strategic planning — an idea he probably would have resisted if presented to him in a vacuum.

Adapting Wall Street to Main Street. The best advisors are able to adapt cutting-edge management techniques to the unique needs of family business. Many families, for instance, are fractured by competing capital demands from shareholders and the business. Growing the business, providing shareholder liquidity and financing ownership succession all can demand significant amounts of cash — sometimes at the same time. (Please see Exhibit 2.) A financial advisor should be able to apply the most up-to-date financing tools to the family business, generating such options as joint ventures, joint venturing or spinning off assets, placing stock privately or creating new classes of stock. Mr. de Visscher, for instance, can help create company-sponsored loan programs, enabling family business shareholders to borrow against their stock at favorable rates of interest. This not only allows shareholders access to cash without selling their stock, but it helps younger shareholders learn financial responsibility with manageable risk. (For more information, please see *Financing Transitions in the Family Business*, No. 7 in the **Family Business Leadership Series**.

6. Initiates periodic meetings with the client for update and review. Good advisors are proactive. They know that a steady flow of information is crucial to offering excellent service, and they often contact the client just to ask what's going on. They also care about implementation of ideas and plans. They follow up to find out whether advice they have given is feasible and to offer mid-course corrections if necessary.

The advisor may suggest meetings several times a year for a status report, an update on key issues and a review of progress, needs and future plans. **And he or she will meet with the business owner annually to assess the past year's relationship and to offer ideas about how the advisor can best help in the coming year. Often, good advisors will**

EXHIBIT 2

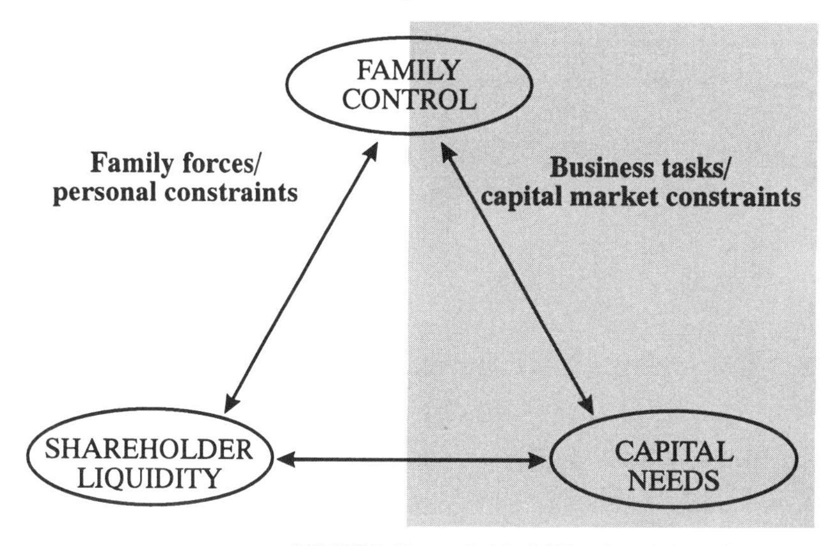

SOURCE: François M. de Visscher, de Visscher & Co.

volunteer at least one new contribution they can make, probably as part of their regular fees.

Good advisors also may suggest that they meet once a year with the management team and the board and make presentations, laying out economic trends as they see them, how the business will be affected, what their role as advisors might be and what new contributions they might make in the coming year. Smaller family businesses may take a more informal approach, bringing advisors and their spouses together annually for a social dinner with the management team and directors to strengthen relationships and build trust.

7. Is resourceful on clients' behalf, spotting opportunities, sharing information and introducing contacts. A good advisor takes the initiative to spot opportunities for the family business. That means offering information, contacts and ideas that can help make the business and the family a success. Without being asked, he or she sends articles, books, reports, seminar information and other items of interest. The advisor creates opportunities for family members and key managers to meet people

TABLE 6

The Special Needs of Family Businesses

Good advisors heed the unique traits of family businesses:

- The need for business owners to make succession, strategic, personal financial and family plans that reflect overlapping business, personal and family goals
- The need to make business goals harmonize with family objectives, philosophies and values
- The need to integrate successive generations of family members with business operations
- In many cases, the need to satisfy shareholder demands for liquidity without relinquishing family control
- In many cases, the need to finance ownership and management succession without relinquishing family control
- The profound impact of family values, history and attitudes on the workings of the business

they should know. He or she also shares ideas and lessons learned from working with many other businesses like yours.

Such resourcefulness can be invaluable in a crunch. Mr. Bock was called by one troubled family to value its businesses and find outside buyers. By the time he arrived, differences among the family members had deepened into an unbreachable chasm. However, Mr. Bock spotted an opportunity the family members had missed. He pointed out a way of preserving family ownership by enabling different family members to gain control of each of three family-owned companies. Pleased at the opportunity to sustain family ownership, the family took his advice and asked him to handle the restructuring.

Good advisors also take the initiative to look beyond immediate questions to long-term issues. When NationsBank's Bruce Miller, vice president of business advisory and valuation services, was asked to provide a valuation of what appeared on the surface as a strong, viable family business, he saw an opportunity to fortify the business still more. The business was dependent on one key manager for all major management functions. Mr. Miller helped the owner put together strategic and successor development plans that helped him begin grooming his three sons and giving each more authority — an effort that has substantially improved the company's bench strength, business prospects and market value.

8. Shows empathy, patience and trustworthiness. Certain personal qualities are crucial in an advisor wrestling with sensitive family business issues.

He or she should be empathetic. "You have to know, to have a feeling for, the relationship between family members," Mr. Bock says. This frees the client to bring up delicate issues.

The advisor needs finely tuned interpersonal skills. Deciding whether in-laws should own stock or what should happen in the event of divorce, for instance, can be uncomfortable. **The skills of the professional advisor can make all the difference in how family members and in-laws perceive topics such as prenuptial and shareholder agreements.**

A good advisor evokes trust. He or she must be "able to lay all the facts on the table and negotiate a satisfactory result. My approach is a very honest approach: These are our problems and how do we solve them?" Mr. Bock says.

Patience with complex family situations is another important trait. Decisionmaking in family businesses is often more deliberate and complex than in widely held or non-family-owned companies, and dependent on family circumstances, Mr. de Visscher says. "That's why it's very difficult for Wall Street to deal with family business," he says. **"It may take one or two years for a family business to reach a decision," and an advisor must be willing to proceed at a pace appropriate to the family's circumstances."**

9. Is willing to work with successor generations. The best advisors see the business longitudinally, anticipating generational transitions and helping clients prepare. Some advisors have relationships that span four generations of family business owners. And they are willing and able to tailor their roles to reflect the changing needs of the business.

An attorney, for instance, may "help prepare the next generation of leadership by teaching them what should be expected of lawyers and how to get that from them," Mr. Krasnow says. A family business consultant may act as a mentor to a successor, providing confidential counsel and arranging learning experiences.

Serving more than one generation can be demanding, requiring the advisor to smoothly make the transition from, say, being a good servant to the founder to being a proactive mentor to the successor. In some cases, successors or shareholder factions may want their own advisors. And as discussed below, an advisor in situations of family tension may be forced by a potential conflict of interest to recommend that family members retain their own advisors.

Barring such issues, **an advisor who manages to cross generational boundaries can fortify family ties for the future and provide a valuable model of flexibility and openness.**

10. Raises questions about the future. Advisors often are the first to raise important questions about the future of the business.

A consultant may alert the business owner to the need for key legal documents, such as buy-sell agreements. A strategic planner or organizational development expert may spot a need for improved family communication or planning for successor development. An attorney or accountant may suggest that trusts be set up early to gift stock to successor generations. A financial advisor may help anticipate future cash needs. An insurance advisor may help guard against unpredictable developments. For example, a business owner may have in place a buy-sell agreement that, in the event of his death, arranges for his son to buy the business from his wife in a series of payments over 10 or 20 years. An insurance advisor, Mr. Blum says, may raise such questions as: Will the business last as long as the payment schedule? Will it have sufficient earnings to make the payments? Will the son continue working in the business long enough to complete the payments?

A banker is often the first person to ask a business owner about his or her succession plan. Though the banker may not be in a position to give tax or estate-planning advice, he or she, acting more as a friend or counselor, "can begin to steer the business owner toward thinking about those things and putting them into perspective from a risk standpoint," Ms. Tubbs says.

Such foresight can be crucial. **Anticipating issues before they command the business owner's attention — and before family members have a chance to form opinions and stake out turf — can make the difference between consensus and turmoil.** "The process is inquiry and exploration of the future," Ms. Wiseman says. "An excellent advisor has more questions than...answers." As the questions are answered, the future becomes more manageable. A good advisor eases transitions to the emerging future state of ownership, leadership and strategy.

11. Promotes collaboration among advisors. An effective advisor should not only be willing to collaborate with other advisors, but should promote it.

As discussed in more detail later in this booklet, a multi-disciplinary team of advisors has the capacity to understand and focus on the business and the family at the same time, says Joseph Astrachan, associate director of the Family Enterprise Center at Kennesaw State College and an experienced family business consultant. Such a group can provide a model for teamwork in the family and generate creative solutions no individual advisor could have come up with alone.

1 + 1 + 1 = 4. The synergy among good advisors can help a family business reach new milestones.

The leaders of one business managed by second- and third-generation family members wanted to buy out inactive family members. The family was cohesive, united by shared values and an appreciation for the founder and his two sons, who still ran the major divisions of the company. But family members active in the business wanted to eliminate the potential for shareholder conflict. They wanted to accomplish this without siphoning off too much cash from the business or "spoiling" third- and fourth-generation holders with a windfall.

The advisory team — an accountant, a family-business consultant and an attorney — had been brought together by the accountant. The attorney and accountant started on the assumption that the buyout would be handled in the usual way: by securing a professional valuation and paying each inactive holder a price based on that valuation, minus discounts for minority interests and a lack of marketability.

But the family-business consultant suggested a different approach. Such a plan could drain large amounts of cash from the business. And calling in a valuation expert could spark family conflict over price, he pointed out. Instead, he suggested using the family's shared values as a foundation for setting a lower price, without calling in a valuation expert.

"Are you sure you're not crazy?" the attorney asked.

Acknowledging that his idea was unusual, the family business consultant insisted, "This family is different." In this group, he said, younger family members might agree to a lower price on the basis of shared goals and values. They might be likely as a group to see the value of preserving family unity and harmony, fostering self-reliance among younger family members or financing continuing growth of the business.

After considerable discussion and research, the advisors found a way to structure a buyout that was legally and financially sound while meeting family goals. To finance the transaction, the business' second-generation owners, who were in their 70s and 80s and financially secure, agreed to give up most of their annual salaries. Based on that added cash flow, they took out a bank loan to finance the buyout. The share price was based primarily on the amount of cash available from the loan. Then, the attorney and accountant provided full and fair disclosure, making sure that all parties understood all aspects of the agreement.

Finally, at a family meeting, the advisory team presented a sizeable disclosure document. The attorney explained the offer, including how the price had been set. The accountant explained the financial dimensions of the buyout. And the family business consultant explained how the proposal reflected family goals and discussed how the conduct of a family business can reinforce important family values. He also addressed such issues as a promise by surviving stockholders that all lineal descendants of the founder would continue to have opportunities to join the business. Moreover, if those family members moved into management, they would again have the opportunity to own stock.

The advisors' presentations set the stage for family members to talk about family values and goals. They reflected on the gift the founder had given successor generations in the form of a thriving business. "In our family, when someone gives us gift, we don't ask what the gift is worth," a senior family member observed. Fourth-generation family members were impressed that "Grandaddy gave up his salary" to offer them cash for their shares.

The buyout was completed — legally, fairly and in harmony with permanently strengthened family values.

12. Gives honest advice even when it may jeopardize the client relationship. In tight situations, there is no substitute for personal commitment by an advisor.

Some advisors may say, "Well, let's try this, and if it doesn't work we'll try something else." That attitude can reflect a lack of conviction, Mr. Nager says. "Advisors should have convictions that they stand by, even at risk of losing you as a client," he says. Adds Mr. Krasnow: "Yes-men" have no role in a well-run business. If you want to hear cheerleaders, go to a basketball game."

A good advisor will not avoid delivering bad news and will strive to do so in a gentle, compassionate way. After working with a longtime client on a succession plan, Mr. Nager sat down with the founder of the business and his wife and told them what they did not want to hear: Their son didn't have what it took to run the company.

Though Mr. Nager knew he risked losing his client, he was able to help the couple accept the truth. And though all three people present shed tears over the outcome of his work, it eventually proved positive for the family and the business. The son was able to admit to himself and his parents that he would rather do something else. And the couple was able to begin the crucial work of grooming a non-family successor.

IV. Red Flags: *Warning Signals in Advisory Relationships*

Just as the attributes described earlier signal benchmark service by an advisor, some behaviors should sound an alarm.

Many advisors agree that certain red flags almost always reflect a lack of professionalism, skill or concern about the client. (Please see Table 7.)

Let's take a closer look.

Conflict of interest. Some conflicts are obvious. Advisors should not work for, or invest in, clients' competitors. (That does not mean that general knowledge of a client's industry can't be extremely helpful.)

Most professionals also see as a conflict of interest any effort by an advisor to sell a client an investment on which he or she stands to profit. While sharing information about investment opportunities may be completely acceptable, making money off a client's investment or loan thrusts the advisor into a new role that can easily conflict with providing objective counsel. At the least, the advisor should divulge, without being asked, any personal interest in ventures he or she recommends.

The advisor also should be sensitive to clients' comfort level over apparent conflicts of interest and discuss them with the client. One longtime client of a bank had decided to split noncompeting lines of the family business between two branches of the family. The bank follows strict confidentiality rules, and there was no actual conflict in the bank's continuing to serve both sides of the family. Nevertheless, to ensure that its clients were comfortable, the lending officer offered one faction — the one that had been first to contact the bank for financing — the opportunity to decide whether the bank should have both branches of the family as clients. When the first group said no, the bank referred the other faction to another lender. "Though we would have felt comfortable banking both of them, we felt it was our obligation to let the client decide," Ms. Tubbs says.

Many professionals believe advisors should avoid owning interests in their clients' businesses. While it may seem convenient and cheap to give an advisor stock, particularly early in the life of a business, it can pose conflicts as the business matures. For instance, an advisor should not be worried about his or her personal financial interests when weighing shareholder liquidity plans or strategic moves that depress the company's value for a while.

TABLE 7

RED FLAGS IN CLIENT-ADVISOR RELATIONSHIPS

A family business owner should examine relationships with an advisor who:

- Fails to avoid conflict of interest
- Fails to respect client confidentiality
- Promotes dependency in a client
- Works primarily in isolation
- Is reluctant to deal with successors
- Sells solutions rather than listening to problems
- Ventures beyond his or her knowledge
- Makes too many decisions for the client
- Fails to foster good communication
- Lacks empathy

Advisors also should not try to put themselves in a position to win a role as a board member or trustee someday. As a general rule, we discourage having advisors serve as members of the board of directors.

Finally, an advisor should be vigilant on the client's behalf to potential internal conflicts. In disputes or occasions when an individual family member's interests diverge with those of the business, an advisor, particularly a lawyer, may need to recommend that the family member retain his or her own counsel. This can be done in a friendly way, stressing the need for different perspectives to be fairly represented. Attorneys are ethically obliged to advise a client "at the moment they see a conflict arising that they feel cannot honestly be mediated without serious consequences for either side," Mr. Krasnow says.

Violating confidentiality. The confidentiality of client information must be respected. A professional should not give out names of clients as a way of winning new clients. References should be disclosed only after they have given permission.

Violations of confidentiality can be disastrous for family businesses.

One family consulted an advisor who subsequently published an article about their problems that too thinly disguised the family's identity. "It produced a family explosion," Mr. Fay says. Anyone who knew the family members recognized them in the story, and the disclosure "crippled family relations so badly that I doubt that the repercussions will subside for a long time," he says.

Family members should not abuse an advisor's obligation to respect confidentiality, either. If one family member asks an advisor not to tell another family member about a substantive issue, there may be an issue of professional ethics, but there also may be "a more subtle and complicated issue of confidentiality," Mr. Horvitz says. "If a husband says, 'Here's what I want to do, but don't tell my wife,'" the advisor must decide where his or her professional obligation lies — with the company and its senior officer, or with all shareholders. On one hand, the attorney may respond, 'You'd better tell your wife to get another lawyer.'" On the other hand, the attorney may comply and risk destroying relationships with other family members who, if they discover the secret, "will never quite trust that person again," Mr. Horvitz says.

Promoting dependency. Any advisor who promotes dependency should be avoided. An advisor should not be possessive of a client nor monopolize the relationship. Such behavior can cause damaging delays in consulting other advisors or solving problems. Also, such self-appointed gatekeepers discourage the collaboration and planning that may be necessary to solve complex problems. For example, a trust officer or other advisor might suggest to a business owner, "Don't worry. If anything happens to you, we'll take care of the business." While a trust officer can provide valuable services and support in the event of a business owner's premature death, he or she should never promote a failure to plan. This only provides a convenient excuse to avoid grooming the next generation for management, finding a non-family successor or, when advisable, laying the groundwork to sell the business.

(While the role of a trust in running a family business is beyond the scope of this booklet, the arrangement should be used cautiously, and often only for a significant but limited period, Mr. Fay says. "Conflicts between competing family and business needs will invariably arise when a family business is held in trust," and the trust should be used to complete, not thwart, the business succession process, he says.)

Conversely, **any advisor who seems too dependent on one or a few clients may mean he or she has nowhere else to turn. The advisor may be so vulnerable to the loss of one client that he or she grows stale and obsequious.** Few advisors in this position are willing to take the risk of challenging a client with new ideas or difficult recommendations — however important they may be.

Working in isolation. Advisors who work in isolation can raise major risks for their clients. No individual, no matter how skillful and technically proficient, can master all the professional knowledge needed to solve some of the most complex family business problems. An advisor must be comfortable at least touching base with other professionals.

"If you have an advisor who is not collaborative, you are doing yourself a disservice," Mr. Nager says. "This is easy to spot. If other advisors suggest a meeting and one says, 'Nah, don't bother to do that. We'll decide when we need to bring in the others. I can take care of that for you,' then that is a clear indication that person is pursuing his own interest, not yours."

One business owner called Mr. Blackman for a second opinion on his will and trust agreement. He had consulted an accountant, an insurance consultant and a lawyer, all expert in their fields, and the documents were well written and professionally prepared. But all the assets, including stock in the business, were held in joint tenancy with his wife — keeping them outside the trust in the event of the business owner's death, and making the combined estates of the business owner and his wife subject to $250,000 in additional taxes. "His accountant planned the business transfer, the insurance consultant suggested the life insurance coverage, and the lawyer did the documents — all experts in their own field, but no quarterback," Mr. Blackman says.

Reluctance to deal with successors. An advisor who resists working with successor generations may be unable to help perpetuate the family business.

Some advisors may feel personally threatened by succession. "When there's a shifting of power" from one generation to the next, some advisors may perceive the change as a threat to his or her livelihood, Mr. Krasnow says. This fear can impede good judgment.

In the best interests of the business, the advisor should rise above personal concerns to help transfer authority and ownership smoothly. To good advisors, "the shifting of power is irrelevant" to his or her primary goal of adding value to the business, Mr. Krasnow says.

Selling solutions. **Advisors who start promoting solutions before they understand the business owner's goals should be avoided.** "The worst case is when an advisor bends a client's plan to what they're good at, or twists every client's problem to fit his formula," Mr. Blackman says. An advisor who sells ESOP plans, for instance, might be helpful under some circumstances. But one who promotes ESOPs as a remedy "for whatever ails you" is probably more interested in making a sale than in helping with your unique problems. In one such case, an advisor eager to set up an ESOP did $75,000 in work for a client before getting a reliable valuation of the company. The business owner was dismayed to learn that the stock's minority interest value in the ESOP was actually worth far less than he had expected. "He had spent $75,000 to learn he was worth only half as much as he thought," Mr. Roberts says.

An advisor may hand out estate-planning advice assuming that the business owner's only goal is to reduce taxes. While reducing taxes may be important, the business owner may also have in mind other goals, such as passing on ownership in a way that promotes harmony among his children or nurtures their leadership abilities.

In an important litmus test, a good advisor "should be listening more than he is talking," Mr. Blum says. "If the advisor isn't listening to the business owner about his life, his business, his concerns, and his children, and what are his real fears about them in the middle of the night — if he is just waiting until it's his turn to talk instead of listening — you have the wrong advisor in front of you," he says. "In this business, winners listen and losers simply wait until it's their turn to talk."

Venturing beyond the advisor's knowledge. A growing number of advisors present themselves as expert in many family-business issues when, in fact, their expertise is narrower. "Family business has become such a tidal wave" that many professionals are acting as specialists even though "it is not appropriate for a lot of them to be in the field," Mr. Blum says.

Erring in this regard can be costly. Relying for a valuation on someone who lacks background in appraising closely held businesses, for instance, "can do significant financial damage" to the legacy you have built over a lifetime, Mr. Miller says. While many advisors "can do a rudimentary job, that doesn't mean the numbers they end up with are correct."

The business owner needs to be aware of each advisor's range of actual expertise and listen carefully when he or she ventures beyond it. While a good advisor will offer all the constructive suggestions possible, **the business owner should discriminate between an advisor's casual opinions and expertise arising from his or her experience.** If a technical advisor offers advice on resolving a sensitive family conflict, for instance, the business owner might respond, "That's very interesting. What leads you to say that?" or, "What kind of experience have you had in such matters?" The answer will help the owner assign the right weight to the advisor's opinions.

Making decisions for the client. Any effort by an advisor to take control of decisionmaking is another warning sign.

While good advisors try to aid decisionmaking and permanently strengthen decisionmaking processes in the family business, they never take charge. If an advisor starts making decisions, "it will quiet things down for a while, but eventually things will start going poorly again," Ms. Wiseman says. "As hard as the decisions may be, they must be made by the people who are living them." Even in the most chaotic situations, she adds, a good consultant should be able to identify the inherent strengths of a family and business and help build upon them.

Failing to foster good communication. Good advisors do not simply talk — they communicate. If your advisor will not explain things to you in clear, simple language, "you should find one who will," Mr. Krasnow says. Any impression that an advisor is not being open or straightforward is cause to examine the relationship.

An advisor should be readily available. If your advisor becomes difficult to reach, stops returning calls or shunts your questions to a junior associate without volunteering a clear and legitimate explanation, you probably should change advisors.

Another red flag is any refusal by an advisor to discuss the cost of his or her services. "Any professional who refuses to talk about it is not the kind of person you would want to hire," Mr. Horvitz says. "Not everybody can say, 'If you have to ask the price, you can't afford it.'"

Lacking empathy. Some advisors are so wrapped up in their knowledge that they fail to empathize with a client's particular situation.

Obviously, there's nothing wrong with being brilliant in one's field, and many successful professional advisors are brilliant. But those who can combine brilliance with empathy for clients are in far shorter supply.

An advisor who lacks empathy may make you feel hesitant to call when you need advice. Why are you reluctant? Is the advisor unpleasant, condescending or uninterested? An advisor's bearing may suggest, "I'm smart and you're paying me a lot of money for my opinion, so if you know what's good for you, you'll take my advice." The advisor may grow impatient when you ask follow-up questions or try to assess aloud the alternatives available to you.

While the advisor's counsel may be technically brilliant, it could also be inappropriate for your personal situation and goals. And simply hearing it may do nothing to help you strengthen your long-term leadership of the business. A great advisor tries to relate to a client's experience and offer help that matches his or her unique needs. Discuss your concerns with the advisor.

V. *Finding and Choosing an Advisor*

■

It takes a wise man to recognize a wise man.

— Xenophanes, "Lives of Eminent Philosophers"

■

Once you know what you want in an advisor — and what you want to avoid — how do you find the right one?

A first step is to define the role you want the advisor to play:

1) Are you looking for a specialist to offer technical expertise on specific questions, such as family compensation, transferring stock to the next generation or adding outsiders to the board?

2) Do you need help defining priorities? This requires a different set of skills, such as interviewing family members and recommending an agenda.

3) Do you need a consultant to lead the problem-solving process? Families sometimes need help improving communication, resolving conflict or picking a successor.

4) Are you seeking a political solution to a problem or a resolution of emotional concerns? A political solution would involve reaching some satisfactory means of divvying up resources, such as buying out someone's stock or creating a new family compensation plan. An emotional resolution might involve counseling, family therapy or training in interpersonal communications. The kind of solution you want should help determine what kind of advisor you call.

Once you have settled on the roles you want, Tables 1 and 2 in this booklet can help you make choices among professional fields. The next step is to begin a search for qualified candidates.

Finding candidates. Searching for an advisor is similar in some ways to looking for a key employee. "Don't go to the Yellow Pages," Dr. Levinson says. **"You have to remember that 50 percent of all professional people were in the bottom half of their class."**

Asking another business owner or a trusted accountant, lawyer, banker or other current advisor for referrals is a good start. When asked, Ms. Tubbs gives names of more than one candidate to help the business owner find a good match. "The business owner needs to find the person who will click with them," she says.

The best advisors often are involved in family business education, making speeches or publishing articles. That means good candidates also can be found through family business newsletters, family business educational programs at colleges and universities, or professional or trade association publications or events. Some business owners "scout" potential consultants before they feel they are needed. They attend seminars and clip articles. They also get involved in university family-business centers to meet people and establish a network of contacts.

Selecting an advisor. A rigorous screening is just as important with advisors as with employees. (Please see Table 8.)

Don't hesitate to call an advisor you don't know for an informational appointment, typically at no charge (unless you hire the advisor and get some work done during the session). You will learn a lot, not only about the advisor but about your business, and the advisor will respect you for it. Through the process, "stay focused on what you want," says Robert L. Heidrick, co-founder of The Heidrick Partners Inc., a search firm. "Does the advisor understand your situation and your problems? If the communication isn't there, it isn't going to work. And if you don't feel comfortable, look elsewhere."

Many family businesses involve key family members in the selection process, inviting two or three advisor candidates to meetings to discuss their background and objectives. In some cases, you might ask for written proposals from candidates outlining their understanding of your business, your needs, how they can help and how you would be charged. Other advisors follow up initial discussions with a less formal letter confirming their understanding of the client's needs and their plans to meet them.

A business owner has a right to expect broad experience. A survey of 18 leading family business consultants by Dr. Astrachan at the Family Enterprise Center showed that most had served between 100 and 400 clients. Most had been consulting in some capacity for more than 20 years. Most had broad experience in resolving conflicts and improving communication, as well as establishing such business policies and practices as an active board, family members' entry into the business and compensation.

Some advisors also believe that professionals who personally have strong family business backgrounds are better equipped to understand family business. "I don't think someone can work with a family business who has not had those kinds of ties," Mr. Bock says. "You need to have the experience of dealing with family business in a very personal way."

If the candidate meets all these criteria, ask him or her for references

TABLE 8

A 12-Point Checklist for Selecting Professional Advisors

- ☐ 1. Do you trust the person and feel confident in him or her?
- ☐ 2. Is the advisor at least as successful in his or her field as you are in yours?
- ☐ 3. Are the advisor and his or her firm growing as ambitiously as you are?
- ☐ 4. Is the advisor still learning and willing to change?
- ☐ 5. Would you be proud to be associated with this person before customers, suppliers and other important contacts?
- ☐ 6. Does the advisor want your business?
- ☐ 7. Is the advisor planning to focus on your kind of business and to grow with those clients? Or would you be a "sideline" or "add-on" to the advisor's primary market?
- ☐ 8. Does the advisor have a good mix of long-term and newer clients?
- ☐ 9. Does the advisor have experience with clients whose family businesses are at least as complex as yours?
- ☐ 10. Does the advisor have a broad enough client base that the loss of any one client would not be damaging? Or would the advisor be substantially dependent on the relationship with you?
- ☐ 11. Does the advisor have enthusiastic references from businesses similar to yours? Have the references given permission to be used?
- ☐ 12. Is the advisor suited to the role you need him or her to play?

and check them out. As discussed earlier, the candidate should either ask the references first for permission or make clear that the references have already given their OK. If this doesn't occur, ask the references whether they gave permission for the business owner to give out their names. If not, the advisor may not be worthy of trust with confidential information.

The references should be in businesses at least as large and successful as yours, and they should be enthusiastic about the advisor's contribution. Ask the references for examples of special contributions by the advisor, how to make best use of him or her, and how the advisor charges for services. Note whether the advisor has many longtime or repeat clients, or if most are new customers.

Professional Accreditations. Business owners often ask about accreditation of family business consultants. While no formal accreditation program exists for specialists in family business, professional and ethical standards for practitioners are a focus of growing attention among people in the field. The Family Firm Institute, Brookline, Mass., a nonprofit association of professionals serving family business, has established a Model Code of Ethical and Professional Guidelines for practitioners that sets standards involving disclosure, confidentiality, conflict of interest, fee structure, integrity and objectivity. The Model Code also sets guidelines for staying current in one's field, conducting research and avoiding discrimination and harassment. A copy can be obtained by writing Judy Green, Executive Director, The Family Firm Institute, 12 Harris Street, Brookline, Mass. 02146; or by calling Ms. Green at 617-738-1591.

EXHIBIT 3

Advice from the Pros

No one has more experience with advisory relationships than advisors themselves. Here are some tips from the pros on selecting an advisor:

"Chemistry and philosophy are even more important than specialization or expertise. You need an individual who has judgment, who can relate well, who is on the same wave length as the family members, who has the same view of the world. The person also needs to be seasoned, and be able to provide what I would call 'old-fashioned counseling' to family members. You need to search for an advisor the same way you would search for a car. Kick the tires and think about it. Sit in the driver's seat and see how it works. See how comfortable you feel."

— Michael Horvitz, Jones, Day, Reavis & Pogue

"The most important thing is to have a feeling that you can work with a person. In my business, it takes six months to a year for a deal to go down. You're going to be in constant contact with one another, and if you don't feel comfortable with an advisor, you shouldn't start a relationship."

— Leonard Bock, Bock, Benjamin & Co.

"A true advisor must be totally independent and able to render advice that is completely unbiased. He should be able to present a set of solutions, and no matter what solution the client picks, there is no different financial reward for Solution A versus Solution B."

— François M. de Visscher, de Visscher & Co.

"You have to understand what you want a lawyer to do and find the lawyer who can do it. If you want a lawyer to pick a fight — to be the snarling vicious bulldog — you sacrifice opportunities. There's no such thing as having a healthy relationship with a pit bull. But if you look at a lawyer as someone who has a series of tools available, including counseling and education, paying the lawyer becomes an investment."

— Henry Krasnow, Krasnow Sanberg & Cohen

"The first thing to ask is, 'Who is going to be in charge of my affairs? Do I have to call different people with different kinds of problems?'

"The second thing to ask is, 'What experience do you have in dealing with family businesses? Don't tell me about closely held businesses. Tell me about family businesses'

"The third thing is, 'What do you know about family systems?'

"No. 4, 'What do you know about the specific problems of business governance in the family business context?'

"And five, 'What professional affiliations do you have that are family business related, and from whom can I get references?'

"Then if the candidate says, 'Here's a list of three family businesses to call,' you might ask, 'How do I know it's okay to call them and that you have permission to disclose their identity?'"

— Michael Fay, Hale and Dorr

VI. *Managing and Evaluating Advisors*

■

"Intelligence is knowing what you don't know. Wisdom is knowing who to ask. Success is the courage to do so."

— A family business owner

■

The arrival of a consultant is too often seen as a panacea.

More often, it means that in-depth work on the business' problems is just beginning.

Making the most of your advisors is a skill that must be honed with effort and experience. Here are some suggestions to help manage your advisors efficiently and well.

Tackle the Issues. A first step toward good management is to overcome any unwillingness to address the problems you face. Some business owners retain a consultant only to keep him or her "on call." This risks letting wounds fester or even losing the opportunity to have senior family members help solve the problem.

Have Realistic Expectations. A business owner should develop realistic expectations of an advisor. If you are asking a consultant for technical expertise on an issue, don't blame him or her for failing to implement a solution. One of the most common pitfalls is to expect a consultant "to solve the problem" or answer the question, "What do we do next?" Instead, the business owner or family should ask, "Can you help us decide how to proceed?"

Be Demanding. Being realistic is not the same as having low expectations. Too many business owners are reticent with professional advisors. They may hesitate to ask an advisor to work hard, spend time or even to explain things in clear language. If you don't understand your advisor, ask for an explanation again and, if necessary, again.

If at first you don't understand what an advisor suggests, it is their fault. But if you don't persist until you do, it is your fault.

Communicate Regularly. It is the business owner's responsibility to keep advisors informed. Some circulate financial reports to their attorneys, insurance advisors and accountants. These reports should not be used by the advisors as an excuse to sell additional services or products, but to stay abreast of the business' needs.

Even if there are no known issues, the business owner also should meet periodically with an advisor or group of advisors and update them with a general discussion of the business and the family. "A good advisor will see opportunities for you in that discussion that he or she wouldn't have recognized otherwise, without knowing what is going on," Mr. Nager says. In one such discussion with a client, an advisor learned in advance about the client's plans to expand into a new region and helped structure the expansion to reduce taxes substantially.

Probe for Suggestions. Don't hesitate to probe a trusted advisor for suggestions. An advisor may withhold valuable ideas if he or she fears the client is unwilling to hear them. If you believe your advisor is holding back some thoughts, open the door for comments.

One entrepreneur was discussing the progress of his son, the heir apparent, with a trusted advisor. "He has been a solid producer now for three years" in a major division of the company, the business owner said.

He paused. Sensing that the consultant was withholding an opinion, he looked up at him. "Maybe he's been there too long," he said tentatively.

"Why not move him around and expose him to different parts of the business?" the consultant said.

"Well, he likes it where he is," the father responded.

"Is just giving him jobs he likes really the best way to prepare him to take over?" the consultant asked gently.

The business owner acknowledged that it wasn't, and the two men went on to discuss how to help the successor break out of his mold and tackle new challenges. They decided on a new role that was central to the business' current strategic goal of cutting costs. The job: a one-year assignment to reduce costs by an amount greater than the son's current bottom-line contribution. To avoid setting the successor up for failure, the target set was smaller than the business owner believed was feasible.

The decision was a major step forward in the successor's development, and one that might never have occurred if the entrepreneur hadn't had the courage to ask his advisor what he was thinking.

Don't Pass the Buck. Some business owners defer to advisors on difficult decisions or details. All too often, for instance, busy business owners strike a deal, shake hands, smile and say, "Our lawyers can work out all the details," Mr. Krasnow says. This often leaves too much negotiating responsibility to someone without real power to make decisions and without a real stake in the outcome. And it can prolong negotiations unnecessarily.

Though working out all the details may be less fun than striking the deal, those details often involve significant business issues that demand the business owner's presence, he says. "Only by attending (and making sure your counterpart attends) every significant negotiation can you be sure that your goals are accomplished," Mr. Krasnow says.

When documents are complete, the business owner again must take responsibility for reviewing them carefully. "It is not your lawyer's responsibility to give final approval to a contract any more than it is your bookkeeper's responsibility to decide how much you will pay your staff," Mr. Krasnow says. You are the only person who understands the business transaction you want and the level of risk you are willing to accept, he says.

Be Open. The more a trusted advisor knows about your business, the more likely he or she is to provide good advice. Ask your advisors whether the information you are giving them is useful and what other information they need.

It also may pay to allow an advisor to have contact with a range of people in the business. Mr. Heidrick frequently helps business owners who know they have "a people problem" but haven't defined the solution. In such cases, he may talk not only with the CEO about the qualities needed in a new recruit, but with others who have helped decide to conduct a search, including the executive committee, operating committee and other senior managers. That enables him to find the right person and therefore, to help define the business' needs. "We don't want to just go out and look for people. We want to understand the environment and be able to explain the role and impact of the position," Mr. Heidrick says.

Managing Advisors in the Organization. If a new advisor is to visit the business frequently or for very long, it is wise to prepare employees and others close to the business.

Employees should be given enough information to understand why a stranger is suddenly spending so much time at the business. If possible, they should understand the goals of the consulting arrangement; otherwise, they may fear the family is preparing to sell the business. And they should be told what information is appropriate to share. Otherwise, they may refuse, out of loyalty to the family, to cooperate with any effort by an advisor to gather information.

Evaluate your advisors. Once you have hired an advisor, do a performance review annually. When appropriate, evaluate your advisors against the benchmarks described in Section III. As part of the evaluation process, interview other advisory firms about every three years. If you are using the right advisors, you won't need to make changes often. But a periodic review can ensure that you don't let inertia take over.

If your advisor is not serving you well, "apply the same management techniques you use in the other aspects of your business when you have an employee or supplier who isn't performing satisfactorily," Mr. Krasnow says. "You either train them to perform to your expectations or find a new one who already has been trained that way."

Managing Teams of Advisors

Business owners often tend to keep advisors apart, meeting with each separately in order to feel more in control.

This divide-and-conquer technique wastes an opportunity to tap the synergy that often develops when skilled and caring professionals come together.

As discussed earlier in this booklet, the complexity of issues facing family businesses often leads advisors to collaborate. "If you get people from more than one discipline all together in a room to work collaboratively, you will get a far better answer than if you use them separately," Mr. Nager says. "When the best advisors work together, you will see magic happen."

Managing teams of advisors presents unique challenges. To foster informal teamwork, give your advisors permission to talk to each other about work they are doing for you and ideas for your business. One family business brings advisors together annually to make presentations at a meeting of family members, key managers and directors. The advisors discuss trends in the economy and the business and the contribution they envision making in the coming year, as discussed in Section III. Another smaller family business brings its advisors and spouses together with family members at an informal annual dinner.

More formal collaborations can take several forms. A trusted lawyer, accountant or other lead advisor may subcontract with other experts to help the family business as needed, Dr. Astrachan says. Assuming the lead consultant is qualified, he or she can oversee the others' activities. In other cases, the business owner may assemble an advisory team. From that group, the business owner or team members need to designate a lead consultant, or the business owner might lead the group. Goals of the collaboration should be clear and ways of resolving differences need to be understood.

It sometimes pays to give a team of trusted advisors joint responsibility for helping make key management decisions. When one family-owned business owner needed a non-family sales and marketing head but felt he lacked adequate experience to make a selection, his family business consultant drew in an executive search consultant, a sales and marketing specialist and a psychologist. Each advisor was given veto power. "If you're not comfortable or have any questions about a candidate, or if any of the advisors don't think it's going to work, let's pass and go on to somebody else," Mr. Heidrick told the business owner. While that approach made the search more difficult, "it assured that we got the right person in the long run," Mr. Heidrick says.

Some business owners worry that advisors will disagree. Remember, if they don't disagree — if all your advisors are telling you the same thing — then some of them are redundant. And conflict may be enlightening for the business owner. An honest dispute among well-intentioned professionals over how to meet your goals will probably result in the best possible solution for you.

One caveat: Do not view your advisors as a substitute for an active board of outside directors. A board of respected peers is different from a group of even the most trusted advisors. Advisors work for you and can always be invited to board meetings. It is not necessary to make them directors to benefit from their knowledge. In contrast, **the ideal director not only has experience running businesses but often has already achieved the goals the CEO is hoping to reach. He or she is a respected peer of the CEO whose position as a director is uniquely designed to foster impartiality, objectivity and clarity.** The director typically does not serve to collect fees, but to learn new things, share problems and look for solutions with a community of peers.

Giving advisors a seat on the board also poses a conflict of interest. One of a board's functions is to help ensure that a business owner is getting the best possible service from professional advisors; that would require an advisor to impartially evaluate him or herself. Another conflict can arise if the board is asked to help evaluate potential successors. A director who is also an advisor may be influenced by worry that a successor will terminate his or her advisory relationship. Many family business consultants avoid becoming directors until after a consultation is complete and the advisory relationship has ended, Dr. Astrachan says.

Managing the Cost of Advisors

Ask your advisors to estimate their expected fees up front and explain all the charges to you. Many advisors provide a written letter of agreement showing projected fees and describing the circumstances under which additional charges would be made. Others reach a verbal agreement with clients in advance.

Whatever the arrangement, no bill should be a surprise. Many advisors offer, without being asked, a detailed projection of their future charges. If a bill is going to be larger than usual, the advisor should warn the business owner and explain why.

If you don't understand a bill, ask for an explanation. Advisors charge for their services in various ways. Some work for hourly, daily or transaction fees. Others work for commissions, and others for a combination of both. You should find out up front what you are paying for.

A financial advisor, for instance, might charge a quarterly retainer or bill on an hourly or daily basis, while the same person might separately charge a flat transaction fee for completing a deal. Some executive search consultants work on a retainer, charging a percentage of the recruit's first-year compensation. Others, particularly those filling lower-level positions, collect a fee only after someone is hired.

The trend in some professions is to charge a flat fee per service rather than an hourly fee. While this method has some advantages, it is controversial in some cases. Many clients perceive it as cheaper to pay, say, a flat $600 for a buy-sell agreement or $10,000 for an executive search, and this approach can be an incentive for advisors to increase their efficiency. On the other hand, flat fees also can be aimed at increasing profit margins. They can provide an incentive for unprofessional advisors to take short cuts or avoid tackling the special complexities of your situation. It also can mean your advisor must press for a deal or a conclusion at all costs to get paid — even if it is a bad conclusion.

Whatever the fee structure, a business owner should be aware that both ways of paying have advantages and disadvantages. In fields such as law, where differences in billing practices exist among professionals, you may want to discuss the issue with your advisor.

The price of good advice. Fees charged by advisors vary widely based on the region of the country and the kind of services rendered. But in one of the few nationwide measures of advisory fees, the survey of 18 leading family business consultants by Dr. Astrachan found that most charge a daily fee, usually for a visit to the client, ranging from $1,500 to $4,000 a day. For shorter periods, such as telephone calls or planning sessions, the consultants typically prorate the same fee to half days or sometimes to the hour.

Retainer Arrangements. Some business owners prefer putting trusted advisors on retainer. Guaranteeing a minimum monthly fee makes some feel more secure in their relationship and more comfortable about calling the advisor frequently. Other business owners may feel they are getting a bargain or "reduced rate" by fixing a monthly fee. They feel liberated from an image of "the meter running" every time their advisor picks up the phone.

Retainer arrangements should be entered with caution, however. If the retainer is a fixed fee, the unprofessional advisor may lack incentive to provide in-depth assistance when a crisis erupts. The business owner may not get his or her money's worth in quiet months.

Other advisors use retainers to protect against misuse of their services. When a client asks for help selling a business, Mr. Bock asks for a two-step payment including a smaller, up-front retainer fee. "This gives us confidence that we have someone who is really interested in selling this company — not somebody who wants us to go out in the marketplace and find out what the company is worth so he can brag about it," Mr. Bock says.

Monitoring Fees. The business owner should be mindful of an advisor's fees on a continuing basis. If every time you call an advisor, he or she uses it as an excuse to try to sell you something or start a costly new project, you probably have the wrong advisor.

Similarly, if an advisor brings partners or co-workers along to a visit or meeting, you have a right to ask the purpose and cost. Some firms do this free of charge to ensure continuing backup service. But if you are to be billed for the extra people's time, ask what benefits that offers you. While it can be extremely valuable to have more than one person in a professional firm know your situation, you shouldn't be expected to finance on-the-job training for your advisor's junior associates that is of no benefit to you.

Managing Advisors with the Family

Family members can play many roles in relation to professional advisors.

They are often involved in deciding to call or in choosing an advisor. At the least, they should be informed before an advisor begins working with the business.

Some business owners call a family meeting to discuss why a consultant is needed and to allow family members to raise any concerns they have about bringing in an outsider. Some families offer members "veto" power over an advisor choice to assure full family support. Family members can hinder an advisor if they refuse to share information or insist that he or she withhold information from other family members. Family members also should be prepared for the likelihood that the advisor will bring about some kind of change.

Many business owners bring family members and advisors together socially, creating opportunities for the advisors to meet spouses or mature children. Others ask advisors to make presentations to family members or to attend annual meetings with directors and the family, as discussed earlier.

If disputes arise, a skilled advisor can operate as a mediator. The mere presence of a respected advisor can encourage family members to behave in constructive, mature ways. The advisor should avoid taking sides; a lack of impartiality is certain to destroy long-term effectiveness.

Consultants' role in relation to family members can be fraught with other pitfalls. A consultant often needs to help resolve tacit disagreements among family members. But the family may feel so threatened by any effort to bring those disagreements out in the open that any consultant who tries may be fired, Dr. Astrachan says. "Creating a safe environment for the discussion of disagreement is a challenging task," he says. As discussed above, having consultants work together as a team can ease some of the tension, by allowing individual consultants to mirror particular positions within the family while working through complex issues together, he says.

Managing Advisors with the Board

Well-managed interaction between professional advisors and directors can yield big benefits for the family business.

Having advisors make presentations to an active board of outside directors can spur the advisors to perform at the top of their form. **Some business owners invite each advisor, one at a time, to present to the board his or her role and insights about the business.** Aware that outsiders on the board are excellent contacts, advisors are likely to present themselves well. They also are less likely to raise fees excessively when they know outside directors are helping oversee their relationship with the business.

Others, as mentioned above, invite advisors to an annual meeting of directors and family members. Most family businesses also have attorneys attend board meetings, to provide advice and to keep him or her informed about the business. A lawyer should not assume he or she is entitled to attend all of every board session, however; the attorney is present at the discretion of the business owner.

VII. *Summary*

A boom in the number of family business advisors has created a big potential resource for business owners.

For the first time, professionals in many fields are tailoring an unprecedented range of skills and expertise to the unique needs of business-owning families. And they are proactively helping business owners plan for future success and family ownership.

Leading a family business can be extremely complex, and every business owner needs professional help from time to time. If advisors are well-chosen, they can help capture opportunities, anticipate transitions, solve problems and resolve conflicts. By drawing on broad experience with other family businesses, they also can protect the business owner from re-inventing the wheel.

While business owners often resist hiring advisors, many of their objections — for instance, that advisors only throw up roadblocks, can't be trusted or wouldn't be interested in their particular problems — often arise from misconceptions or experiences with poorly qualified advisors.

This booklet establishes some benchmarks for excellent advisory service. Good advisors not only have strong technical knowledge, but understand the business and the family and the complex ways they relate to each other. Their advice suits both the business and the family. They are empathetic, patient and trustworthy. They raise important questions about the future of the business. They help spot opportunities. And they adapt cutting-edge management and financing techniques to the unique needs of each family business, helping to permanently improve strategy and decisionmaking processes. **Working collaboratively with the family and other advisors and providing honest, empathetic, straightforward counsel, good advisors also can provide a valuable model of clear communication, teamwork and commitment.**

Conversely, some behaviors by advisors should raise red flags for the business owner. Failing to avoid conflict of interest or to respect client confidentiality, promoting dependency in a client, failing to listen and respect a client's goals and values, or failing to foster good communication are all warning signals that something is wrong in an advisory relationship.

Once the business owner knows what to look for, selecting the right advisor becomes a deliberate and careful process. First, the immediate role you want the advisor to play should be defined. Is technical expertise needed? Do you need help defining priorities? Do you need help with the process of solving a problem? Once these questions are answered, the business owner should conduct a search no less rigorous than looking for a key manager. Candidates should be carefully screened, interviewed and checked out. And fees, confidentiality concerns and other potentially sensitive issues should be discussed up front.

After advisors have been selected, the relationship requires ongoing management. A willingness to tackle the issues and probe for solutions; strong communication, and high but realistic expectations are important to sustaining a productive relationship. **Encouraging advisors to team up on tough problems can yield even greater returns, as the synergy among committed professionals often generates creative ideas no one of them could have produced alone.**

These techniques can foster benchmark advisory relationships that will leave both your business and your family permanently stronger.

APPENDIX
Guide to Contributors

Joseph Astrachan, Associate Director, Family Enterprise Center, Kennesaw State College, P.O. Box 444, Marietta, GA 30061. Telephone 404-423-6045. An associate professor of management and entrepreneurship at Kennesaw State College's Coles School of Business Administration, Dr. Astrachan is associate director of Kennesaw State's Family Enterprise Center, a member of the board of directors of the Family Firm Institute, and an experienced family business consultant, author, speaker and editor.

Irving L. Blackman, Partner, Blackman Kallick Bartelstein, 300 South Riverside Plaza, Chicago, IL 60606. Telephone 312-207-1040. A certified public accountant and attorney, Mr. Blackman is the founding partner of Blackman Kallick Bartelstein. He specializes in transfer, succession and estate planning issues affecting closely held businesses. He frequently speaks and writes on those topics and sits on the advisory boards of several family-owned businesses. He also is the author of ten books, most recently *Transferring the Privately-Held Business* (Probus Publishing Co., Chicago, Ill., and Cambridge, England, 1993).

Joseph F. Blum, CLU, J.F. Blum & Associates, 1 Pond Park Road, Hingham, MA 02043. Telephone 617-749-7700. Fax 617-749-8780. An agent for Massachusetts Mutual Life Insurance Co., Mr. Blum specializes in insured succession and estate plans for family businesses. He is founder and chairman of the Northeastern University Center for Family Business, Boston, and spearheaded MassMutual's Family Business Initiative. Mr. Blum also has written numerous articles for trade journals and family business publications on "how to maintain control while letting go."

Leonard Bock, Principal and Co-Founder of Bock, Benjamin & Co., Monarch Plaza, 3414 Peachtree Rd., Suite 730, Atlanta, GA 30326. Telephone 404-816-0049. Mr. Bock's firm arranges private placements of debt and equity and represents owners on an exclusive basis in the divestiture of their businesses. The principals have completed more than $1 billion in transactions, including 74 divestitures on behalf of clients in the service, retail, distribution, manufacturing and health care industries. Previously, Mr. Bock was founder and president of Bock, Center, Garber, Long (est. 1984), where he specialized in mergers, acquisitions and corporate finance for middle market businesses.

François M. de Visscher, President, de Visscher & Co., 130 Mason St., Greenwich, CT 06830. Telephone 203-629-6500. Fax 203-629-6547. Mr. de Visscher's firm is an independent financial advisory and investment banking concern that designs and implements financial solutions to the liquidity and capital needs of families in business. He is the former managing director and founder of the family business group at Smith Barney, Harris Upham & Co. Inc., New York, and has experience as an investment banker and an accountant. Mr. de Visscher also is actively involved in his own family business, a multibillion-dollar steel wire manufacturer now in its fourth generation of family ownership.

Michael L. Fay, Senior Partner and Co-Chairman, Family Business Practice Group, Hale and Dorr, 60 State Street, Boston, MA 02109. Telephone 617-526-6320. Fax 617-526-5000. Mr. Fay advises clients with respect to a wide range of concerns faced by family businesses, including financial structures, issues relating to business governance and control, succession planning and its effects on family relations, and disposition of family business enterprises. He also serves as a professional trustee, and deals with an array of issues affecting estate and business planning for individual and family clients.

Robert L. Heidrick, Co-Founder of The Heidrick Partners Inc., 20 N. Wacker Drive, Suite 2850, Chicago, IL 60606-3171. Telephone 312-845-9700. Fax 312-845-9822. A former vice president, marketing, for American Hospital Supply Corp., Mr. Heidrick started working in the executive search business in 1975 and started his own search firm, Robert Heidrick Associates, in 1977. In 1982, he organized The Heidrick Partners with his father Gardner, co-founder and former chairman of Heidrick & Struggles Inc., a Chicago-based search firm. The Heidrick Partners specializes in nationwide searches for senior executives and directors, maintaining a proprietary database of director candidates.

Michael J. Horvitz, Partner, Jones, Day, Reavis & Pogue, North Point, 901 Lakeside Ave., Cleveland, OH 44114. Telephone 216-586-7170. Fax 216-579-0212. As director of privately owned business for the firm's tax group and co-chairman of the firm's private business and investment team, Mr. Horvitz specializes in tax-oriented business and commercial transactions, including acquisitions, leveraged buyouts and venture capital financings. He is experienced in advising clients on the relationships among shareholders and partners, as well as on charitable planning.

Henry C. Krasnow, Krasnow Sanberg & Cohen, 10 East Erie St., Suite 300, Chicago, IL 60611. Telephone 312-654-0654. Fax 312-654-0580. An attorney and certified public accountant specializing in representing family and other entrepreneurial businesses, Mr. Krasnow has published numerous articles and lectures to business owners to help them get more value from their lawyers. He also teaches MBA candidates at the Illinois Institute of Technology's Stuart School of Business.

Harry Levinson, Chairman, The Levinson Institute Inc., 404 Wyman St., Suite 400, Waltham, MA 02154. Telephone 617-895-1000. Fax 617-895-1644. Dr. Levinson is a clinical professor of psychology at Harvard Medical School and head of the Organizational Mental Health section of the Massachusetts Mental Health Center. In a distinguished career that spans more than four decades, he has been affiliated with the Harvard Graduate School of Business Administration, the Massachusetts Institute of Technology, the Ford Foundation, and other institutions. He created and for 14 years directed the Industrial Mental Health division of the Menninger Foundation. A consultant and lecturer, he is the author of many articles and books on the psychology of executives, corporate leadership, careers and management.

Bruce Miller, Vice President and Senior Analyst, Business Advisory and Valuation Services, NationsBank Corp., 600 Peachtree St. NE, Suite 800, Atlanta, GA 30308. Telephone 404-607-4539. Fax 404-607-6512. Mr. Miller performs independent valuations of closely held businesses in a wide range of industries for business owners, attorneys, accountants and fiduciaries. He has primary responsibility at NationsBank for valuing closely-held corporations, partnerships, notes and other intangibles for estate and gift tax purposes, sale transactions, corporate recapitalizations, buy-sell agreements and employee stock-ownership plans. He frequently speaks and lectures to professional audiences and trade groups on valuing the closely held business and has written articles for professional publications.

Ross W. Nager, Executive Director of the Arthur Andersen Center for Family Business and Worldwide Director of Family Wealth Planning, Arthur Andersen & Co., 711 Louisiana, Suite 1300, Houston, TX 77002. Telephone 713-237-2323. Fax 713-237-5668. Mr. Nager coordinates the firm's family and closely held business activities worldwide. A nationally recognized advisor in family business succession planning, Mr. Nager has worked extensively in planning for families and closely held businesses in virtually all industries. He is immediate past chairman of the Estate and Gift Tax Committee of the American Institute of Certified Public Accountants.

John R. Patterson, Senior Vice President, Investment Management, Estate Planning and Business Advisory Services, NationsBank Corp., 600 Peachtree St. NE, Suite 800, Atlanta, GA 30308. Telephone 404-607-4550. Mr. Patterson provides extensive estate planning services to family businesses throughout the country, working with NationsBank specialists in tax planning, business valuation, real estate and investment management.

Jim Roberts, President, Management Planning Inc., 101 Poor Farm Road, Princeton, NJ 08540. Telephone 609-924-4200 or 216-861-1555. Fax 609-924-4573. Management Planning has specialized in the preparation of independent, supportable valuations of close corporation securities and partnership interests since 1939.

Linda Tubbs, Senior Vice President and Manager, Portland commercial banking, First Interstate Bank of Oregon, 1300 S.W. Fifth Ave., Portland, OR 97201-2753. Telephone 503-225-2496. Fax 503-225-4698. Ms. Tubbs is responsible for eight lending offices that market bank services and lend to corporations in Oregon and southwestern Washington. Her 22-year career in banking includes forming and managing the Oregon Corporate Division at First Interstate, which markets bank services to companies with more than $50 million, and managing the head office Corporate Banking Center as a senior vice president. She is a member of the Advisory Board for the Oregon State University Family Business Program and a Senior Fellow in the American Leadership Forum.

Kathy Wiseman, President, Working Systems Inc., 2000 L Street NW, Suite 522, Washington, DC 20036. Telephone 202-659-2222. Fax 202-785-9735. A specialist in organizational and leadership development in small businesses, including family firms and entrepreneurial startups, Ms. Wiseman has extensive experience in challenging organizations and leaders to greater effectiveness and productivity. Before 1984, she was a consultant at the American Center for the Quality of Work Life and W.P. Dolan Associates, Kansas City, MO, where, as part of a team, she worked with unions and managements to help them improve quality of work life and productivity. Ms. Wiseman also is an associate of the Georgetown Family Center where she develops and facilitates programs on individual and organization effectiveness based on family system theory. She was elected president of the Family Firm Institute in 1994.

Index

Accountant 2, 5, 13, 28, 29, 30, 39, 46
Accounting firm 13, 18
Advice, why business owners don't seek it 1
Advisor candidates 39, 40-43
  finding 39-40
  interviewing 40, 48
Advisor/client relationship warnings 32
Advisor/director relationships 52-53
Advisor/family relationships 51-52
Advisor selection 49
  12-point checklist 41
  qualifications 55
Advisors, objections to hiring 55
Advisors, outgrowing 11
Advisors' personal family business backgrounds 40
Advisory quality, determining 22
Advisory service benchmarks 15-30
Advisory team 28, 29, 30
  assembling 48-49
Annual meetings 52
Annuities 3
Arthur Andersen & Co. 13, 21, 22
Arthur Andersen Center for Family Business 60
Asset buyers, identifying 3
Astrachan, Joseph 29, 40, 48, 49, 50-51, 52
Attorney 2, 5, 13, 18, 19, 21, 27, 28, 29, 30, 32, 46, 48, 53
Authorship 40
Banker 2, 5, 13, 28, 39
Behavior patterns 21
Bingham, Barry Sr. 9, 10
Bingham family 9
Bingham, Sally 9, 10
Blackman, Irving L. 17, 18, 34, 57
Blackman Kallick Bartelstein 18, 57
Blum, Joseph F. 17, 28, 35, 57
Board of directors 2, 48
  outside board members 39, 40, 49
Bock, Benjamin & Co. 42, 57-58
Bock, Leonard 15-16, 26, 27, 40, 42, 51, 57-58
Bridge managers 2
Business advice, general 2
Business goals 26
Business governance policies 2
Business growth, financing 2
Business issues, anticipating 28
Business opportunities 26
Business owner attitudes toward advisors 9-13
  demands on advisors 11
Business ownership, perpetuating 2, 3

Business purchasers, identifying ... 3
Business, revitalizing ... 2
Business stages ... 1, 5-7
Business-family understanding ... 16
Buy-sell agreements ... 2, 20, 21, 28
Capital needs ... 3, 1824, 25
Capital structure ... 2
Client Confidentiality ... 32, 41
  violating ... 32
Client goals ... 55
Client meetings ... 16
Client relationships ... 30
Client values ... 55
Cohesiveness ... 3
Collaboration among advisors ... 16, 48-49, 55
Collaborative spirit ... 34
Commitment to advisory field ... 15
Communication ... 3, 16, 17, 18, 28, 32, 39
  clarity of ... 17
  fostering ... 2, 36
  improving ... 40
  regular ... 46
Compassion ... 30
Compensation planning ... 2, 20, 39
Competitors ... 31
Compromise ... 2
Conflict ... 12
Conflict of interest ... 27, 31, 49
Conflict resolution ... 1, 2, 3, 40
Contract negotiation ... 2
Corporate structure ... 2
Costs, managing ... 50
Cousins ... 1
Daughter ... 21
de Visscher & Co. ... 18, 25, 43, 58
de Visscher, François M. ... 18, 27, 43, 58
Debt placement, private ... 3
Debt placement, public ... 3
Debt repayment ... 3
Debt-equity ratio ... 2
Decision making process ... 36
Defining advisory roles ... 39, 55
Demands on advisors ... 45
Dependency, promoting ... 32, 33, 55
Disability protection ... 3
Disclosure by advisors ... 30
Dividend policies ... 3
Educating family members ... 16
Emotional concerns, determining ... 39
Empathy ... 16, 27
  lack of ... 32, 36
Employees, meeting with ... 17
Employment policies ... 2

Enthusiasm . . . 16
Entrepreneurial business phase . . . 1
Entrepreneurs . . . 10
ESOP plans . . . 35
Estate planning . . . 2, 3, 9, 10, 17, 28
  understanding goals of . . . 35
Ethical & Professional Guidelines, model code of . . . 42
Evaluating advisors . . . 45
Excellence in advisors . . . 16
Executive search consultant . . . 2, 6, 49
Executive search firm . . . 40
Expectations, realistic . . . 45
Experience with family businesses . . . 19, 40
Family & organizational development consultant . . . 12
Family business case studies, using . . . 19
Family business conferences . . . 19
Family business consultant . . . 2, 3, 7, 20, 29
Family business education, involvement in . . . 40
Family business expertise, scope of . . . 35
Family business insights, multilevel . . . 21
Family business needs . . . 26
Family business newsletters . . . 40
Family business, passing on . . . 13
Family business professionals, recognizing . . . 19
Family business programs, college & university . . . 40
Family business transitions . . . 15
Family conflict . . . 10, 35
Family counseling . . . 39
Family dynamics . . . 17, 20
Family dynasty phase . . . 1
Family Enterprise Center . . . 29, 40, 57
Family Firm Institute . . . 42
Family goals . . . 26, 30
Family history . . . 26
Family meetings . . . 2, 52
Family members . . . 51
  entry into the business . . . 30, 40
  inactive in the business . . . 1, 29
  meeting with . . . 48
Family mission statements . . . 2
Family partnership . . . 20
Family partnership phase . . . 1
Family statements of purpose . . . 2
Family systems theory, understanding . . . 19, 23
Family therapy . . . 39
Family tree . . . 18
Family values . . . 26, 29, 30
Fay, Michael L. . . . 18, 33, 43, 58
Fees . . . 12, 36, 50-51
  discussing . . . 36
  managing . . . 12, 50
  monitoring . . . 51
  retainer . . . 50-51

Financial advisor 3, 6, 7, 24
Financial advisory firm 18
Financial interest in client business, avoiding 31
Financial plans 26
  personal 2
Financial responsibility, learning 24
Financial statements 2
Financial systems 2
Financing Transitions in the Family Business 24
First Interstate Bank of Oregon 11, 60
Foresight 28
Formula solutions 20
Gatekeepers 33
Green, Judy 42
Growing the business 24
Growth potential 18
Hale & Dorr 18, 19, 43, 58
Heidrick Partners Inc., The 40, 58
Heidrick, Robert 40, 47, 49, 58
Honesty 30
Horvitz, Michael J. 13, 15, 33, 36, 42, 58
How Families Work Together 18
Industry knowledge 15
Information sharing 12, 47, 52
Insurance agent 3, 6
Insurance policies, explanation of 3, 17
Interpersonal communications training 39
Interpersonal skills 27
Interview style 18
Investment banker 3, 5, 6
Investment banking firm 18
Investment disclosures by advisors 31
Investors, identifying potential 3
IRS audits 10
Isolation, working in 32
J.F. Blum & Associates 17
Jones, Day, Reavis & Pogue 12, 42, 58-59
Kennesaw State College 29, 57
Key managers 13, 23
Krasnow, Henry .... C. 10, 27, 30, 32, 36, 43, 47, 48, 59
Krasnow Sanberg & Cohen 10, 43, 59
Law firm 13, 18
Lawsuits 10
Lawyer *(see Attorney)*
Levinson, Harry 12, 18, 22-23, 39, 59
Levinson Institute, The 12, 59
Life insurance advisors 17, 28, 46
Limits 32
Lines of credit 2
Liquidity demands 2
Listening skills 35, 55
Litigation 2
Loans 2

Louisville Courier-Journal . . . 9
Management decisions, making . . . 49
Management issues . . . 12
Management Planning, Inc. . . . 9, 10, 60
Management, professionalizing . . . 2
Management succession, financing . . . 26
Management techniques, adapting . . . 24
Management transfer . . . 34
Managers, evaluation of . . . 3
Managers, key . . . 48
  meeting with . . . 17
Managing advisors . . . 45
  in the organization . . . 47
Marketability discount . . . 29
Massachusetts Mutual Life Insurance Co. . . . 9, 11, 17, 57
Mediator . . . 52
Mentor . . . 2
Miller, Bruce . . . 26, 35, 59
Minority interest discount . . . 29
Misconceptions . . . 55
Multi-disciplinary teams . . . 28, 29
Multigenerational service . . . 27
Multigenerational view . . . 27
Nager, Ross W. . . . 13, 20, 21, 22, 24, 30, 34, 60
NationsBank Corp. . . . 1326, 59-60
Networking . . . 19
Non-family executives, incentives for . . . 3
Non-family managers . . . 3
  recruitment of . . . 2
Office visits . . . 17
Opinions, discerning . . . 35
Organizational development expert . . . 3, 6, 28
Owner attitudes . . . 26
Ownership restructure . . . 3
Ownership succession, financing . . . 26
Ownership transfer . . . 34
Participation in the business . . . 20, 21
Patience . . . 16, 27
Patterson, John . . . 13, 60
Peer . . . 49
Performance standards . . . 10
Personal goals . . . 26
Plant visits . . . 17
Prenuptial agreements . . . 27
Proactive stance . . . 24
Problems as planning catalysts . . . 23
Professional accreditation . . . 42
Promotion policies . . . 2
Proposals, written . . . 40
Psychologist . . . 12, 49
Publicly-traded stock price . . . 9
Questions, open-ended . . . 18
Questions, raising . . . 28

References 32, 41
  providing 19
Referrals 39
Relationship warnings 31-37
Reputation 16
Resourcefulness 25
Roberts, Jim 15, 35, 60
Screening advisors 40
Selling formula solutions 34
Shareholders 30
  agreements 27
  buyouts 2, 3
  conflict 9, 10, 29
  liquidity needs 3, 24, 25, 26
Siblings 1
Solutions, nontechnical 19
Solutions, political 39
Solutions, technical 19
Speechmaking 40
Spouses 48
Stock buyout 29, 30
Stock, classes of 24
Stock, gifting 28
Stock, transferring 39
Stock ownership 20
Stock placement, private 3
Stock placement, public 3
Stock restriction agreement 2
Strategic plans 26, 28
  developing and implementing 2
Stress 18
Succession 10, 12
  financing 2
  planning 2, 17, 26
  plans, developing and implementing 2
Successors 2
  candidates 22
  dealing with 34
  development 3, 28
  financial education 2, 3
  instruction of 2
  grooming 26, 33
  non-family 30
  selection 3, 39
Suggestions, probing for 46
Systems Theory 16
Tackling issues 45
Tax planning 2, 28
Tax returns 2, 18
Teamwork, building 3
Technical expertise 15, 39, 55-56
Trade association appearances 40
Transition 18

Trust officer 7, 33
Trusts 20, 28, 33
Trustworthiness 10, 16, 27, 41
Tubbs, Linda 10, 28, 39, 60
Undervaluing advisors 12
Unity, fostering 2
Valuation expert 15, 29
Valuation of business assets 3
Value-creation potential of business 18
Veto power 52
Wall Street 27
Wall Street investment banking firm 15
Wiseman, Kathy 12, 21, 28, 36, 60-61
Working in isolation 34
Working Systems Inc. 12, 60-61

The Authors

Craig E. Aronoff and John L.Ward have long been recognized as leaders in the family business field. Founding principals of **The Family Business Consulting Group**, they work with hundreds of family businesses around the world. Recipients of the Family Firm Institute's Beckhard Award for outstanding contributions to family business practice, they have spoken to family business audiences on every continent. Their books include *Family Business Sourcebook II,* and the three-volume series *The Future of Private Enterprise.*

Craig E. Aronoff, Ph.D., holds the Dinos Distinguished Chair of Private Enterprise and is professor of management at Kennesaw State University (Atlanta). He founded and directs the university's Family Enterprise Center. The center focuses on education and research for family businesses, and its programs have been emulated by more than 100 universities worldwide. In addition to his undergraduate degree from Northwestern University and Masters from the University of Pennsylvania, he holds a Ph.D. in organizational communication from the University of Texas.

John L. Ward, Ph.D., is the Ralph Marotta Professor of Private Enterprise at Loyola University Chicago. He teaches strategic management and business leadership at Loyola's Graduate School of Business, and is a regular visiting lecturer at two European business schools. He has previously been dean of undergraduate business at Loyola and a senior associate with Strategic Planning Institute (PIMS Program) in Cambridge, Massachusetts. A graduate of Northwestern University (B.A.) and Stanford Graduate School of Business (M.B.A. and Ph.D.), his *Keeping the Family Business Healthy* and *Creating Effective Boards for Private Enterprises* are leading books in the family business field.

the center and the woman standing there with the Pipe were Lakota adaptations from the Sun Dance (Mooney 1896: 915). However, as Powers indicates, the Ghost Dance was foreign to Oglala religious ideology: "Although the ghost dance was prematurely aborted with the massacre at Wounded Knee, it is unlikely that it would have survived much longer in its particular form" (1977:202). Here we see an unsuccessful interaction between Lakota and pan-Indian identity.

The next pan-Indian movement was Peyote, which followed the Ghost Dance by only fourteen years on the Pine Ridge Reservation. It should be noted in passing that Omer Stewart is critical of any causal relation between the spread of Peyote and the Ghost Dance (1972). From one viewpoint, what later became the Native American Church was very successful on the reservation. The Lakota put their own traditional stamp on the Half Moon fireplace in Red Bear's use of the Pipe at the time of origin on the reservation and throughout the years with Hawkins, Gap, and now Solomon Red Bear, Jr., the great-grandson of the first Red Bear. In addition, the four smokes with the ceremonial cigarette standing for the Pipe, the four water calls, the roadman going out of the tipi to pray in the four directions—all show how elements of the Half Moon fireplace had a strong continuity with traditional Lakota identity. The result is that the Native American Church acquired a Lakota identity without losing its pan-Indian one. But this very presence of a strong traditional identity has also influenced most Lakota to be satisfied with their Lakota religion. In a 1968 Baseline Study among those surveyed, only 7.5 percent said that they had attended Peyote meetings (10 percent full-bloods and 6 percent mixed-bloods) and only 0.8 percent claimed the Native American Church as their primary religious affiliation (Pine Ridge Research Bulletin 1969:5). I would estimate that the active members on the reservation never exceeded 350 in number.

Social dancing, called powwow celebrations, are events which bring many different tribes together. Although not religious, these events bring a sense of pan-Indianism to more tribes throughout the country than any other movement or activity.

The most recent pan-Indian movement is the American Indian Movement [AIM]. It is one that brings conflict and tension. These include national goals vs. reservation ones, anti-Christian vs. Christian attitudes in Lakota religion, tribal sovereignty vs. tribal government, the Sun Dance as a pan-Indian ceremony vs. a tribal one, and the deepening of full-blood and mixed-blood conflicts. Occupying Wounded Knee in 1973 for 71 days may have been good for national goals but, in my opinion, it lost the tribal election for Russell Means, one of the Lakota AIM leaders. AIM was an outside force called in to remove the mixed-blood Tribal President and even to abolish the entire system of Tribal Government. There is also confrontation between AIM members and the established medicine men over the presence of Christianity in traditional Lakota religion, which will be developed below. The presence of AIM has produced conflict within the Lakota identity which must be worked out in the years to come. Despite this, the Lakota have influenced AIM through the Pipe and the Sun Dance. I think that the Sacred Pipe as a religious symbol and the Sun Dance as a religious ceremony have regained their importance as a source of pan-Indian unity, an importance which may at one time have been eclipsed by Peyote.

Howard's study of pan-Indianism among the Oklahoma tribes helps our understanding. According to him, pan-Indianism among these tribes resulted from the loss of tribal identity and a failure to achieve sufficient acculturation into white society: "rather than becoming nondistinctive members of the dominant culture, many Indians have instead become members of a super tribal culture which we term pan-Indian" (1955:215). The main social expression of this new identity was the powwow and the main religious one was Peyote. Howard concludes: "Pan-Indianism is, in my opinion, one of the final stages of progressive acculturation, just prior to complete assimilation. It may be explained as a final attempt to preserve aboriginal culture patterns through intertribal unity" (1955:220). On the Pine Ridge Reservation, some Lakota fear AIM may be a force weakening the strong tribal identity rather than a help in preserving it due to an overemphasis on pan-Indianism and nativism.

The second complexity from without comes from the Lakota relating to the white man's world. Powers correctly states that there is a continuum between the Lakota and the white man's world. He comments:

> The majority of the people living in the mid range move back and forth along the continuum situationally. At the white man's end of the scale

> they observe technology and change. But at the Oglala end they see ideology and continuity. There they find a connection with the past expressed in the concept of *wakan,* that which is sacred, but also that which is old. The continuity extends back into time long before the European arrived. Those who wish to be part of this continuous stream will move towards the Oglala end, consciously or unconsciously. Sometimes it is mere curiosity which brings an Oglala back to his traditions; sometimes it is illness of a sort, a symbolic illness for which no medical practitioner has a remedy at the white man's end of the continuum (1977: 205–6).

I quote this partly because it expresses so beautifully the Lakota identity which is the basis of their religious life, but also to point out an oversimplification. Powers is also stressing the psychological persistence to the detriment of the acculturational modifications. There are times when a Lakota goes back to his end of the continuum and finds it lacking. The spirits involved in traditional Lakota religion today, as in the past, are at one time a source of strength and at another time one of fear. According to McGee, their "adoration expressed fear of the evil rather than love of the good" (1897:1840). And Mooney states that Black Coyote had to obey a voice "somewhat resembling the cry of an owl or the subdued bark of a dog, demanding" that he cut out seventy pieces of his flesh to appease "an overruling spirit" so that more of his children would not continue to die (1896:898). Another deficiency was the vague and unconvincing belief in life after death in the Lakota tradition, which was treated above. The Lakota Christian who believes in the Resurrection of Christ has a greater sense of continuity with his basic human needs and desires in the traditional Christian church on the white man's end of the continuum than he does in his own Lakota tradition. People famous in Indian religion, such as Black Elk and all the present-day medicine men, receive their Christian sacraments and burials. I think it is more correct to say that the Lakota identity, just like anyone else's, is frequently ambivalent—containing both feelings of continuity and discontinuity with basic human needs, of security and insecurity, of strength and fear.

And when a Lakota does go back to his end of the continuum, he does not always go back to a pure Lakota identity but to one that has been modified by Christianity. And when he selectively returns to the white man's end, he returns to a Christianity that has been modified by Lakota tradition, so that in fact the distance between the two ends becomes shorter. The Oglala Lakota identity is indeed complex, but it is the only solid foundation upon which their religious life can be based.

A MODEL OF OGLALA RELIGIOUS IDENTITY

The following model relates the mutual dynamics of the three religious traditions—represented by Pipe, Bible, and Peyote—which are a part of the contemporary Lakota identity. These three traditions result in six religious groups. *Group* is a general and perhaps vague word; here it is used in the sense of "an assembly of persons who are considered as one or acting as one" because a more appropriate word cannot be found. The American Indian Movement is considered a movement; the Body of Christ Church and Native American Church, Cross Fire fireplace, are definitely churches; the Half Moon fireplace can be considered a church but more vaguely than the Cross Fire; Ecumenist I and II are traditional Lakota people sharing a common attitude towards Christianity. In the field these groups have clearly determined boundaries even though they defy classifications.

These identities will be summarized here. However, they will become clearer in the discussion that follows.

The Pipe alone represents a Lakota identity as conceived primarily but not exclusively by AIM: that is, based upon traditional Lakota symbols having acquired a nativistic value.

The Bible alone represents a Lakota Christian identity as conceived by the Body of Christ Church: that is, based upon a rejection of Lakota religious symbols. This apparent contradiction will be treated below. The Bible alone does not represent the identity of the traditional Christian churches, since in this study this identity is associated with the Pipe or Peyote or both.

The Pipe and the Bible represent a unified Lakota Christian identity as conceived by those in the Ecumenist II, based upon Lakota religious symbols that have acquired a Christian value. The Ecumenist I group is considered an imperfect stage of the Ecumenist II one. Those in this position have a split Lakota/Christian identity, which results in

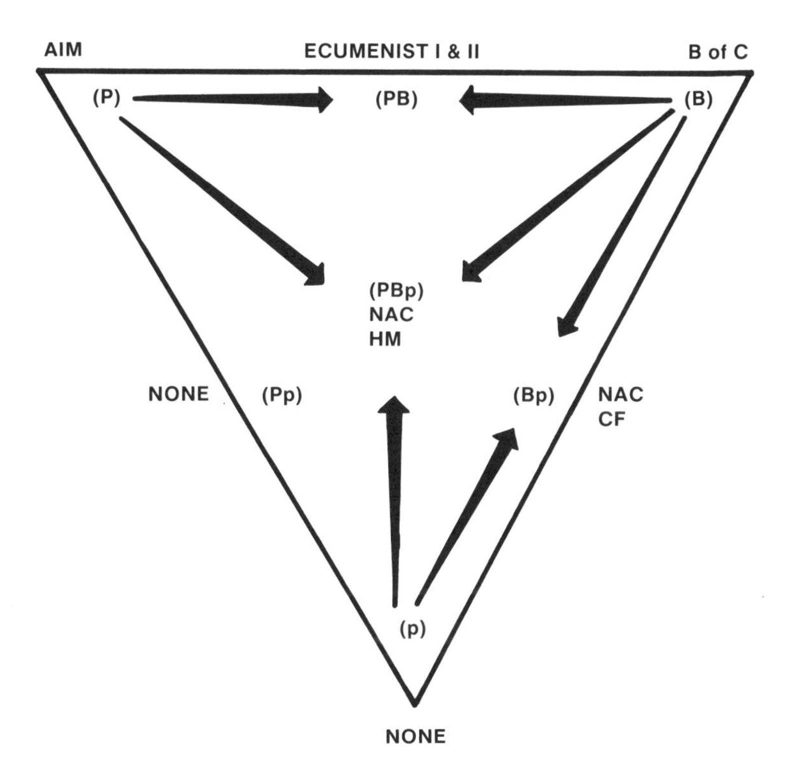

AIM = American Indian Movement
B of C = Body of Christ Independent Church
NAC, CF = Native American Church, Cross Fire Fireplace
NAC, HM = Native American Church, Half Moon Fireplace
(P) = Pipe; (B) = Bible; (p) = Peyote

their moving back and forth on a religious continuum between Lakota and Christian ends.

The Bible and Peyote together represent a unified Lakota Christian identity as conceived by the Native American Church, Cross Fire: that is, based upon Peyote's receiving an explicit Christian value, the Bible being placed upon the Peyote altar.

Pipe, Bible, and Peyote together represent a unified Lakota Christian identity as conceived by the Native American Church, Half Moon: that is, based upon Peyote's acquiring a new value through both the traditional Lakota and Christian religious symbols. (This is true even though the Bible itself is not brought into the meeting.)

Peyote would have represented the Lakota identity as conceived by the Half Moon without any association with the Pipe and the Bible.

The Pipe and Peyote together would have represented a Lakota identity as conceived by the same group without an association with the Bible. But since conditions are not verified, there are no religious groups in these positions.

The members of these six groups discover their own characteristic meanings in Pipe, Bible, and Peyote. For example, among these groups, with the exception of the Body of Christ, the Pipe has a common meaning shared by all (developed in the second chapter). These values will not be repeated here but only the ones characteristic of each group. These characteristic values could be considered as configurations in Ruth Benedict's meaning of the word (1936).

The American Indian Movement

One characteristic value of AIM is militancy. This is in keeping with Lakota tradition, as the Pipe was the center of the warrior societies. Wissler describes each society as having a Pipe bearer (1912). McGee states that the Sioux had a tomahawk Pipe that stood for either war or peace; this was part of the Sioux mentality (1897:172). Kroeber brings out the purely symbolic nature of these Pipes. The tomahawk Pipe of the eastern Indians was a metal hatchet with a bowl and a wooden handle which was also a stem; accordingly, the hatchet could be used either to chop or to smoke. The pipestone imitations of the Sioux could not be actually used to chop, so that this aspect was only symbolic (1948:480). We can recall the warlike associations with the Sun Dance. This part of the Lakota tradition, which was suppressed in the acceptance of passive resistance, is being revived today. On some occasions the Pipe is not the Peace Pipe but the war Pipe, uniting the Lakota in militant activity.

Another characteristic value is tribalism. One resolution of an International Treaty Council, held at Kyle, South Dakota, during the summer of 1978, was to "discourage whites from trying to take our religion, not understanding it, playing with our pipe and our sacred things, and trying to put on their own sun dances" (*Rapid City Journal* 1978). In this regard, we can recall the Lakota woman complaining of my presence at Green Grass during the Calf Pipe ceremony. This expresses the AIM viewpoint that Lakota religion is to be shared with no one outside the tribe. Although secrecy is a traditional aspect of Indian religion, AIM members' understanding of the Pipe involves a "new ethnicity," a concept discussed at the 1973 conference of the American Ethnological Society: "one dominant theme in these papers on identity would appear to be boundary maintenance, or, at any rate, the need to define ethnic self always in the context of some outside group" (Bennett 1975:6).

Tribal sovereignty is yet another characteristic value. AIM members claim that, according to treaty, the Oglala Nation has absolute sovereignty. Another resolution of the International Council held at Kyle was to "discourage immigration to our reservation." This claim was dramatized during the occupation of Wounded Knee by declaring the little hamlet a sovereign nation before the television cameras. This declaration is similar to the Ghost Dance expectations of complete sovereignty. One young medicine man believes in tribal sovereignty but not by violence, since in some way God will give sovereignty to the Indian people. At the Sioux Treaty Hearings held in Lincoln, Nebraska, during December of 1974, the AIM lawyers unsuccessfully attempted to dismiss the criminal charges against some of the participants in the Wounded Knee occupation on the grounds that the U.S. Government did not have jurisdiction on the Pine Ridge Reservation because of tribal sovereignty (Ortiz 1977: 13).

The Pipe is also a symbol of pan-Indianism. This was very noticeable on the Longest Walk from San Francisco to Washington, D.C., participated in by a large number of tribes from all parts of the U.S. The Pipe was carried on foot over three thousand miles—even through snowstorms in the southwestern mountains. Here we see the Lakota tradition of always carrying the Calf Pipe used. One Lakota commented that if the march accomplished nothing practical in Washington, it did bring many different tribes together in a common venture and created a sense of solidarity. The Indians were also allowed to swear on the Pipe instead of the Bible in the treaty hearings just mentioned (Ortiz 1977:10). Since the Pipe was shared by many tribes from all over the country, its pan-Indian identity was again prominent.[1]

Another characteristic value of the Pipe is an anti-acculturation and anti-Christian one. Vine Deloria raises some legitimate questions concerning the relation between Indian religion and Christianity (1973); Vernon Malon and Clinton Jesser discuss the conflict in values which took place between these two religious traditions among the Lakota (1959). However, AIM members reject any integration of Lakota and Christian traditions, a relationship described by Jorgensen and Clemmer as "that old will of the wisp 'acculturation through syncretism' at work. We are led to believe that the Indian religion is moving toward the real (Primitive) Christianity through the inevitable acculturation process" (1978:43). The error in this attitude is the attempt to keep a traditional Lakota religion static, forgetting that all traditions must be changing. For the mature adult, even enculturation involves cultural change, as is reflected in the definition: "Enculturation is the learning process by which man, throughout his life, acquires his own culture. . . . Thus enculturation in infancy (usually on an unconscious level) is a mechanism favoring cultural stability, whereas enculturation in the mature individual (involving conscious acceptance or rejection of new forms of behavior) is important for cultural change" (*Encyclopedia Britannica* 1974, Micropedia: 887)

The final characteristic value is nativism in Linton's sense as "any conscious organized attempt on the part of society's members to revive or perpetuate selected aspects of its culture" (1943:230). This is seen primarily in reviving what was lost. An appeal to the now defunct societies of the past (Wissler 1912; Blish 1926: 1934) as a source of the ethical values needed to live a true Lakota life today is an example of revivalistic tendency. Perhaps, AIM could be classified primarily as a revivalistic and secondarily as a perpetuative nativism. In my opinion, nativism is the most basic characteristic value, of which the other values are expressions.

The Body of Christ Independent Church

As we have seen, the Body of Christ is a small Pentecostal Christian Independent Church. Their fundamental interpretation of the Bible influences their concept of Lakota identity. They do not consider their church a white man's church, and yet they reject all traditional Lakota religious symbols as a means to true Lakota identity. We gain an insight into their understanding of Lakota identity, although expressed in terms of Indian identity, from a sermon which a visiting Kiowa minister from Oklahoma delivered in one of their services at Wolf Creek. (Parentheses indicate reactions from the congregation.)

"People try to say: 'Brother Keith, I'm an Indian,' but, brother, you better get rid of that Indian way. You better get rid of that Indian. (Applause.) And you better let the love of God begin to come into existence in a way as the Lord says: 'there is neither Jew nor Greek nor slave.' There is only the children of God. I am proud to be an Indian, but when I repent of my sins, when Jesus came with the Holy Ghost, I became proud of the fact that I am a son of God, that I had lost my identity, that Jesus took on the identity in my life. Sure, when I hear that old tom-tom beating, the old Indian inside me resurrects again, but I have to put him down—keep him under subjection and say 'no' because it is of the world. (Yes, O Jesus.) When I listen to my uncles singing Peyote songs in the Kiowa language, that old Indian inside of me, that old Kiowa inside of me, tries to raise his head but, brother, I got to put him down. I have to say: 'get behind me, Satan,' because it is just the old natural man, the old carnal man trying to raise himself up again. (Yes, it is.)"

The applause which occurred when the preacher urged them to get rid of the Indian should be noted. The mentioning of the "old Kiowa" after the "old Indian" inside of him is an example of pan-Indian shifting to tribal identity. But most important is the fact that this is an expression of a transcultural religious identity which is neither traditional Lakota nor white: in their minds a newly conceived Lakota identity, divorced from any Lakota religious identity and rejecting all Lakota religious symbols. This is expressed through Biblical allusions. According to their viewpoint, yuwipi is the work of the devil. Visions of men and animals are an illusion. The Pipe is compared to the golden calf the Hebrews worshipped in the desert. When faced with the problem of the Lakota Christian's relation to his past religious tradition, their solution is one of rejection.

However, Lakota associations are part of their church. The main Body of Christ community is a Lakota *tiospaye,* or extended family—the Black Feathers and other families married into them. Other Lakota associations include healing through supernatural means; visions, but not derived from the Lakota world; and conversion through an experience of power. What attracts Lakota to the Body of Christ Church is their feeling that the power of Christ is superior to the power of the Pipe: but an experience very different from the one that Black Elk had in his conversion, as will be seen below.

There is also a pan-Indian identity. The members have an evangelical spirit that leads to missionary activity among other Indian tribes. They go out from Wolf Creek to North Dakota, Canada, and other places to conduct revival meetings. This activity develops a strong awareness that their commitment to Christ is not just Lakota but for all tribes.

I feel there is no need to point out the features common to any evangelical Pentecostal-type Church. The Body of Christ Church fulfills the needs of its members through a deep religious experience of commitment to Christ. It has an important contribution to make to the study of acculturation, since it is an example of Christianity being a dynamic force in the life of full-blooded Lakota who are unacculturated in all areas of their life except religious symbolism. Although their rejection of Lakota religious identity is bound to have adverse psychological effects, it is possible that the Bible as a power in the traditional Lakota sense (as Densmore's informants and Sword experienced it), may be a sufficient mediating symbol between their Lakota and Christian identities. Their traditional understanding of power did make the Lakota open to new religious influences. However, we shall see that the Lakota Ecumenist II acceptance of traditional Lakota religious symbols would seem to be a much more appropriate solution, avoiding the misunderstandings of the Body of Christ's fundamentalism. But the fact that they are deeply dedicated and not superficial Christians runs contrary to the experience of Hallowell's "superficially acquired Christianity" among the Ojibwa (1955:112).

The Lakota Ecumenist II Group

Thomas W. Overholt in his article on the Ghost Dance states that "the phenomena of Indian conversion to Christianity and of Christian elements in native ceremonies are complex and interesting, and can't be discussed in detail here" (1978:193, n. 25). The detailed discussion below will be a critical attempt to fill in this gap in scholarly research. It will perhaps help clarify "a certain ambiguity in Black Elk's feelings about his power and the fate of his people" (Overholt 1978:180).

Sun Dancer walking between the dancing.

Frank Fools Crow piercing a dancer.

Frank Fools Crow taking a pierced dancer to his dancing position.

Pierced dancers.

George Plenty Wolf bringing in ceremonial food after the Sun Dance ceremony.

The people thank the Sun Dancers at the conclusion of the ceremony.

Benjamin Black Elk at the grave of his father, Nicholas Black Elk,
at Manderson, S.D.

Benjamin Black Elk offers the Sacred Pipe in Our Lady of the Sioux Catholic Church at Oglala, S.D.

Jake Herman and Edgar Red Cloud

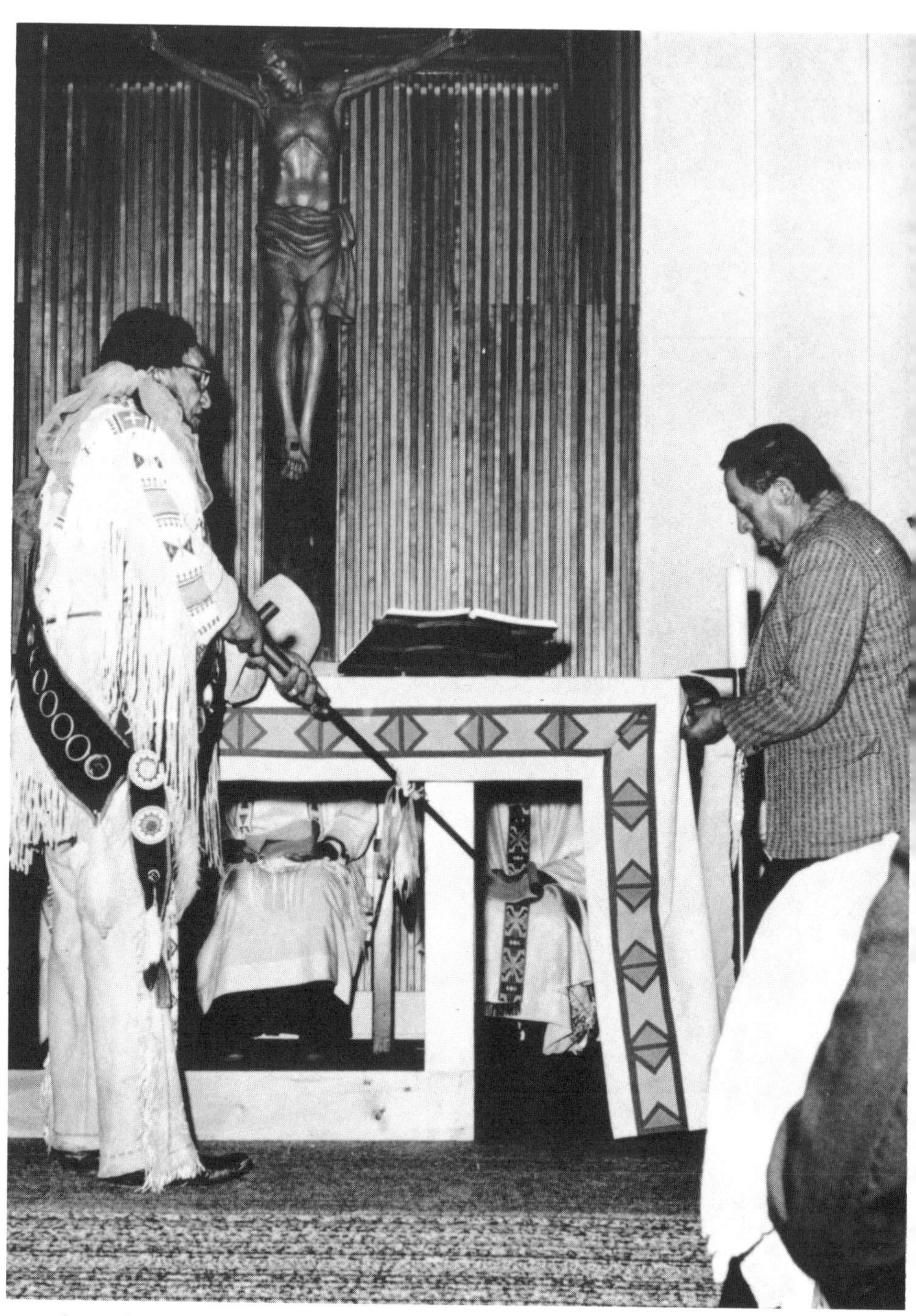

Frank Fools Crow praying with the Sacred Pipe at the dedication of St. Isaac Jogues Catholic Church in Rapid City, S.D. (Courtesy of the Archives of the Diocese of Rapid City, S.D.)

Father Paul Manhart, S.J., making the Sacred Pipe a symbol of death.

The author praying with the Sacred Pipe in Sacred Heart Church, Pine Ridge, S.D.

The contribution of the Ecumenist II group is in showing us how Christian religious symbols were implied and dimly grasped in the earlier Lakota ones. Eliade gives us an example in the Cross taking the place of the Cosmic Tree, being "conditioned by the very structure of the symbol of the Cosmic Tree" at the same time it "extends and perfects the idea of cosmic *renovatio* symbolized by the World Tree."

> All this could be formulated in another manner. Symbols are capable of being understood on more and more "elevated" planes of reference. The symbolism of darkness allows us to grasp its meaning not only in its cosmological and initiatory contexts (cosmic night, prenatal darkness, etc.), but also in the mystical experiences of the "dark night of the soul" of St. John of the Cross. . . . But then one may ask if these "elevated" meanings were not in some manner implied in the other meanings, and if, as a consequence, they were, if not plainly understood, at least vaguely felt by men living on archaic levels of culture. . . . The difficulty of the problem rests on the fact that symbols address themselves not only to the awakened consciousness, but to the totality of the psychic life. . . . This admitted, two important consequences follow:
>
> 1. If at a certain moment in history a religious symbol has been able to express clearly a transcendent meaning, one is justified in supposing that this meaning might have been already grasped dimly at an earlier epoch.
> 2. In order to decipher a religious symbol not only is it necessary to take into consideration all of its contexts, but one must above all reflect on the meaning that the symbol has had in what we might call its "maturity" (1959:106–7).

From the Lakota Christian viewpoint in the Ecumenist II group, this maturity is Christ. However, those Lakota in the Ecumenist I position simply see common religious forms in the two religious traditions. In answer to Bruce Forbes' criticism that I am moving "beyond description and interpretation to an advocacy of the Ecumenist II position" (1985:86), I feel that I am discovering the Ecumenist II viewpoint in their religious imagination and not projecting my own onto it, even though I did advocate this viewpoint in my work among them.

Powers claims that seeing the Sacred Pipe as a foreshadowing of

Christ "is more about religious imperialism than empirical reality" (1986:118). The truth is that Power's rejection of this concept is a form of anthropological imperialism in which an anti-Christian bias does not allow him to see the empirial fact that Christianity had a significant influence on Lakota religion. Plenty Wolf accepted me as a Catholic priest praying with the Sacred Pipe. At least one time he believed that the power of the priest was stronger than his own power as a yuwipi man. In the late 1960s his granddaughter had an epilepsy attack. When the young girl was brought to him, he said that he did not have power over this and that she should be taken to the priest to be prayed over. There is no doubt that his respect for me as a priest increased when I prayed with the Sacred Pipe and that it, in turn, received a special meaning. The ample documentation below will show that some Lakota did have the faith to believe that Christ was the fulfillment of the Sacred Pipe.

In another place Powers makes unfounded assertions and prejudges the motives of a priest:

> Historically and traditionally we would tend to interpret this use of native materials [offering up a sacred pipe and wearing beaded vestments] by a Catholic priest as strategy designed to win converts through a kind of moral deception, one deemed acceptable because the stratagem would ultimately lead to a civilized revelation rather than a primitive vision. But would we ever be willing to admit that the priest believed in the efficacy of the pipe? Were the trappings of native religion now part of his religious system?
>
> Historically we must answer no. . . . We would agree, I think, to accept the priestly overtures as a stratagem of the Catholic Church, which, in the words of the Jesuits, "uses the best of any culture for its own advantages (Holy Rosary Mission 1963:20)" (1987:99).

Powers is talking about my praying with the Sacred Pipe, beginning in 1965. He had no way of knowing my intentions. My intention was to establish the Sacred Pipe as a sacramental in Catholic ceremonies. Although this gives the Pipe a new meaning, it in no way destroys its Lakota one. I certainly believe in the efficacy of the Pipe derived from both the Lakota spirits and Christ. I certainly never considered the Sacred Pipe as "the trappings of native religions." Powers simply assumes I have this negative attitude. We can recall Emerson Spider defending my praying with the Pipe in the Native American Church meeting. Below, we will see how many Lakota medicine men accepted this practice of mine. I wrote that the Catholic Church "uses the best of any culture for its own advantage" a quarter of a century ago, before my thought had matured. I would qualify this statement today, although there is a sense in which it is still true since, through the inculturation of the best of Lakota religion, the Catholic Church is better off. None of the medicine men, including George Plenty Wolf (whom Powers regards very highly) accused, or even suspected, me of moral deception. Powers is treating the whole process of inculturation very superficially, without any understanding.

Powers also shows his lack of understanding about the presence of Christianity among the Lakota in viewing its effects as restricted to its social functions. It is true that "as a means of survival and adaptation to the unalterability of the white man's dominance, Christianity has been used in such a way that old cultural institutions and their associated values may persist under new labels" (1987:124). But to claim that Lakota religion satisfies religious needs and Christianity social ones is simply being blind to the facts (1987:123). It is Christianity and not Lakota religion that at times of death is the primary source of strength for the vast majority of Lakota people. Lakota meditate on the Bible and receive the sacraments for religious needs and not social ones. But, of course, Powers is unfamiliar with these matters, for he has not spent any time serving the Lakota people in religious ministry.

Kaiser shares the same anti-Christian bias in making the old worn-out accusation that "Holy Men and traditional Lakotas practiced Christianity to please their conquerors" (1984:19). As we will see below, there was genuine conversion in the lives of Black Elk, Plenty Wolf, and other Lakotas on the Pine Ridge Reservation. Kaiser becomes very judgmental in stating that "some Catholic priests began feeling the need to make Christianity more relevant to the Lakotas, perhaps because they thought that more relevance would finally loosen the Lakotas' retention of old beliefs" (1984:19). I enhanced the Sacred Pipe in the eyes of the Lakota Christian by making it a sacramental sign of Christ not to suppress the Lakota religious tradition but to make it a permanent expression of Christianity. For a Christian to do this is to recognize the validity of Lakota religion.

The best starting point for an understanding of this relationship is

Black Elk's Messiah vision, which he received while participating in the Ghost Dance. I will quote from the Neihardt fieldnotes, published by Raymond DeMallie, since they contain material left out of his *Black Elk Speaks*—material which is essential in my discussion.

"As I landed there, I saw twelve men coming toward me and they stood before me and said: 'Our Father, the two-legged chief, you shall see.' Then I went to the center of the circle with these men and there again I saw the tree in full bloom. Against the tree I saw a man standing with outstretched arms. As we stood close to him these twelve men said: 'Behold him!' The man with outstretched arms looked at me and I didn't know whether he was a white or an Indian. He did not resemble Christ. He looked like an Indian, but I was not sure of it. He had long hair which was hanging down loose. On the left side of his head was an eagle feather. His body was painted red. (At that time I had never seen any picture of Christ.)

"This man said to me: 'My life is such that all earthly beings that grow belong to me. My Father has said this. You must say this.' I stood there gazing at him and tried to recognize him. I could not make him out. He was a nice-looking man. As I looked at him, his body began to transform. His body changed into all colors and it was very beautiful. All around him there was light. Then he disappeared all at once. It seemed as though there were wounds in the palms of his hands (DeMallie 1984:263).

"It seems to me on thinking it over that I have seen the son of the Great Spirit himself. All through this I depended on my Messiah vision whereas perhaps I should have depended on my great vision which had more power and this might have been where I made my great mistake" (266).

My first observation is that Black Elk is reflecting on his vision as a Lakota Christian, having been a Catholic catechist for close to twenty-eight years. His reflections involve an explicit knowledge of Christ. Secondly, the man in the vision was initially the Ghost Dance *Wanekia* ("savior") and not the Christ of his Catholic faith since Black Elk had nothing to do with the white man's religion at the time. He seemed to have acquired little knowledge of Christianity on his European trip in the Buffalo Bill show. The Christian message was not an explicit one for Black Elk but rather an intimation. Although the

Ghost Dance is a syncretism of Indian and Christian elements, Black Elk did not recognize it as such. On the level of phenomenology, Black Elk experienced a Messiah manifestation, but it was only later—after his conversion—that the Ghost Dance Wanekia would be recognized as the Son of the Great Spirit Himself in the sense of Christ. This discovery was the result of Black Elk's groping toward the Messiah's identity after his conversion to Christianity. At first he said that the man "did not resemble Christ. He looked like an Indian." And here Black Elk received his first lesson as a Lakota Ecumenist. For in later reflection he came to the conclusion that this man was the Son of the Great Spirit, proving that his preconceived assumption about Christ—that He could not be an Indian—was wrong. And to Black Elk, who knew Christ as a catechist, the signs must have been so obvious, reminding him of Christ in the transfiguration on Mount Tabor and the risen Christ showing the wounds of the nails in the palms of His hands.

In *Black Elk Speaks* Neihardt is misleading when he has Black Elk saying: "I heard the gossip that was everywhere now, and people said it was really the son of the Great Spirit who was out there; that when he came to the Wasichus [white man] a long time ago, they had killed him; but he was coming to the Indians this time" (1961:239). Black Elk actually told Neihardt: "From the rumors and gossips I heard this Messiah was the son of the Great Spirit that had come out there" (DeMallie 1984:258). But this is simply the name and title given to the man Wovoka (256–57), and there is no indication in the field notes that Black Elk identified the Ghost Dance Messiah with Christ at this point in time. The first mention of Christ in the field notes is when Black Elk reflects upon his Messiah vision after he had become a Catholic catechist.

And so the man he first recognized as the Ghost Dance Wanekia was now identified as the Christ of his Catholic faith. Black Elk then expresses a doubt. He is not sure whether following the Messiah vision instead of his first vision of the flowering tree was a mistake or not. And in my mind another question arises. Does his statement "all through this I depended upon my Messiah vision" refer to before or after the recognition of the Ghost Dance Messiah as Christ? Which vision is it that lacked power—the one in which the man was recognized only as the Ghost Dance Messiah or the one in which he was recognized as Christ? One thing is certain: a Lakota Christ has come to Black Elk in a Lakota vision.

I believe that Black Elk's vision dramatizes the starting point for the Ecumenist II position. Black Elk had an intimation of the presence of Christ of which he was only vaguely aware yet which produced an intense fascination. Only after Black Elk had explicitly known Christ could he realize that he had actually seen Him without knowing it. And this is what the Lakota Ecumenist does—discovering the presence of the unknown Christ in his Lakota tradition, since he is reflecting on this tradition from the viewpoint of his Christian faith.

A young medicine man relates what a man around ninety-one years old and living at Green Grass told him. The man said that after the White Buffalo Woman brought the Pipe, a white man came dressed in a buffalo robe. He spoke Lakota and blessed the Pipe. This was Christ Who came in the spirit before the white man brought Him. The young medicine man comments: "At the time that Christ died, the woman brought the Calf Pipe. When the Pipe was brought, there was a vision of a white man before they ever saw one. He was Christ coming in spirit to the Indian people at the same time that He was born among the white man. This is the reason the Indian respected the white man when he first came. This is the reason why I respect all the Christian Churches."

The association of additional symbols will give us a deeper understanding. The red pipestone is the blood of the Indian people. Catlin gave the reason for the Indian's alarm at the white man's discovering the Pipestone quarry in Minnesota: "As this red stone was part of their flesh, it would be sacrilegious for the white man to touch or take it away. . . . a hole would be made in their flesh and the blood could never be made to stop running" (1844:126). According to Sword, the shaman filled the Pipe and said, "Spirit Pipe, we smoke this pipe to you" (Walker 1917:126). Eagle Feather gives the Spirit Pipe of Sword a meaning that corresponds to the Ghost Dance Messiah of Black Elk before he recognized Him as Christ: "The Peace Pipe or Sacred Pipe is a very important part of the [Sun Dance] ritual and is used because the Traditional Sioux of modern times sincerely believe that it is our Jesus Christ, or our Saviour, and that He is still here on earth in the person of the Pipe. The non-Indians have killed and crucified their

Saviour. This is why traditional people do not celebrate Easter at all" (Mails 1978:88). On the level of phenomenology, Eagle Feather is recognizing the same religious meaning of saviour in the Lakota Pipe and in Christ, which is the Ecumenist I position. Black Elk went beyond this in recognizing the Ghost Dance Messiah as Jesus Christ Himself.

I would like to return to Black Elk's conversion to Christianity, because in it there is yet another example of the Lakota religious experience of power. Black Elk experienced power in the traditional Lakota world. John Lone Goose, who was the Catholic organist at Manderson and worked with Black Elk as a catechist, states:

"I first met Nick around 1900, when I was a young boy and he was not a Catholic. I don't know what they call him in English, but in Indian they call him 'yuwipi' man. Sam Kills Brave, he's a Catholic, lived close to him. And before Nick converted, Kills Brave would say: 'Why don't you give up your yuwipi and join the Catholic Church? You may think it best, but the way I look at it, it isn't right for you to do that yuwipi.' Kills Brave kept talking to him that way and I guess Nick got those words in his mind. He said that after Kills Brave spoke to him, he wanted to change" (Steltenkamp, n.d.).

This information is confirmed by a Lakota man in his sixties who grew up as a boy in Manderson. He told me that people expressed surprise when Black Elk became a Catholic catechist, since he had been a yuwipi man. These same people described the yuwipi meetings Black Elk had conducted. Although Neihardt does not describe any of Black Elk's curing ceremonies as yuwipi, neither does he do so for Chips, who was certainly yuwipi (1961:77).

It is against this background that we can appreciate the following testimony of Lucy Looks Twice. "That's when in 1904 my father was called to doctor a little boy in Payabya, seven miles north of Holy Rosary Mission. The boy's family wanted my father to doctor their son because they heard he was good at it. So my father walked over there carrying his medicine and everything he needed for the ceremony. At that time they walked those long trails if they didn't have a horse.

"When he got there, he found the sick boy lying in a tent. So right away, he prepared to doctor him. My father took his shirt off, put tobacco offerings in the sacred place, and started pounding on his drum. He called on the spirits to heal the boy in a very strong action. Dogs were there and they were barking. My father was really singing away, beating his drum and using his rattle when along came one of the Blackrobes, Fr. Lindebner, Ate Ptecela (short Father). At that time the priests usually traveled by team and buggy throughout the reservation. That's what Ate Ptecela was driving.

"So he went into the tent and saw what my father was doing. Fr. Lindebner had already baptized the boy and had come to give him the last rites. Anyway, he took whatever my father had prepared on the ground and threw it all into the stove. He took the drum and rattle and threw them outside the tent. Then he took my father by the neck and said: 'Satan, get out!' My father had been in the 101 [Wild West] show and knew a little English so he walked out. Ate Ptecela then administered the boy communion and the last rites. He also cleaned up the tent and prayed with the boy.

"After he got through, he came out and saw my father sitting there downhearted and lonely, as though he lost all his powers. Next thing Fr. Lindebner said was "come on and get in the buggy with me." My father was willing to go along and so he got in and the two of them went back to Holy Rosary Mission. . . . My father never talked [i.e., normally] about that incident but he felt it was Our Lord that appointed or selected him to do the work of the Blackrobes. You might think he was angry, but he wasn't bitter at all.

"He stayed at Holy Rosary two weeks preparing for baptism and at the end of those two weeks he wanted to be baptized. He gladly accepted the faith on December 6, 1904, which was the feast of St. Nicholas. So they called him Nicholas Black Elk. After he became a convert and started working for the missionaries, he put all his medicine practice away. He never took it up again.

"My father said that what he was doing before he met Ate Ptecela was the work of the Great Spirit but that he suffered a lot in doing it. As a matter of fact, he had ulcers and had to be treated for them shortly after he started his missionary work. The Jesuits sent him to a hospital in Omaha and he was on a diet for two or three months until his ulcers cleared up. When he converted, knowing about Christ was very important to him and receiving communion was what he really held sacred.

"People who used to be treated by him when he was a medicine man started coming to him. They asked him about the new church he belonged to and he explained to them what it meant. Many followed his example and he instructed them in the new faith.

"[Steltenkamp continues] Stated most simply, according to Lucy, the only factors pertinent to her father were that (1) a holy man was present, (2) the holy man's power was known to be very strong, (3) resistance to such powers was unthinkable, and (4) Black Elk regarded his power as negligible by comparison. Her father had 'suffered a lot' while practicing as a medicine man and had experienced what might be called 'spiritual restlessness.' Lucy further mentioned that once her father undertook the work of a catechist, his ulcers were never again bothersome. Black Elk clearly felt that the 'Son of God had called him to lead a new life.' The Christian Lord Black Elk heard spoken of during the Ghost Dance times had 'selected him' to do his work.

"John Lone Goose adds one further comment: 'he never talked about the old ways [i.e., in his days as an active catechist]. All he talked about was the Bible and Christ. I was with him most of the time and I remember what he taught'" (Steltenkamp, n.d.).

Looks Twice's last remark is contrary to the Neihardt manuscript. It is certainly possible that she is projecting a later Christian meaning back to that time.

Black Elk's life as a Catholic catechist did require him to suppress traditional Lakota religion much of the time into his unconscious, which surfaced in the Neihardt and Brown interviews. It was the personal image of Christ in his Messiah vision that was a mediating symbol, in a Jungian sense, resulting in an integration of the two religious traditions on a deep emotional level.

Yet, it was by no means a total suppression. Black Elk did consciously integrate the two religious traditions in a remarkable way. The image of the Ghost Dance Messiah did surface into consciousness. According to Frank Fools Crow, "Black Elk was very interested in the teachings of the Roman Catholic Church, and spent many hours talking to priests about it. When he and I were discussing it one day, Black Elk told me he had decided that the Sioux religious way of life was pretty much the same as that of the Christian Churches. . . . We could pick up some of the Christian ways and teachings, and just work them in with our own, so in the end both would be better" (Mails 1979:45). Fools Crow's remark brings out both sides of Black Elk's life. When he "spent many long hours talking to the priest," he suppressed his Lakota religion. However, in private conversations, he consciously brought the two together. Fools Crow believes in Black Elk's position and in the mutual benefits both religions receive from each other. I don't question which religion was superior in Fools Crow's mind. When he became sick during the 1980 tribal Sun Dance and retired to his tent, he asked me to give him the Sacrament of the Annointing of the Sick and Holy Communion on the Sun Dance grounds. He did not ask for one of the Lakota medicine men to pray over him.

DeMallie brings out the same conscious inculturation. Commenting on Black Elk's teaching on the Sacred Pipe, DeMallie says that "these teachings seem to represent the end point in Black Elk's synthesis of Lakota and Christian beliefs, for in them he structures Lakota rituals in parallel fashion to the Catholic sacraments. Perhaps this was Black Elk's final attempt to bridge the two religious traditions that his life had so intimately embodied" (1984:71).

This explains why the very expressions that Black Elk uses in *The Sacred Pipe* show a Christian influence.

> Any man . . . who is attached to the senses and to the things of this world, is one who lives in ignorance and is being consumed by the snakes which represent his own passions (Brown 1953:4n). . . . It should also be a sacred day when a soul is released and returns to its home, *Wakan-Tanka* (8). . . . Further, my relatives, our Father, *Wanan-Tanka,* has made His will known to us here on earth, and we must always do that which he wishes if we should walk the sacred path (13). . . . and as the flames of the sun come to us in the morning, so comes the grace of *Wakan-Tanka,* by which all creatures are enlightened (71). . . . I think I should explain to you here, that the flesh represents ignorance and, thus as we dance [in the Sun Dance] and break the thong loose, it is as if we were being freed from the bonds of the flesh (85).

These expressions are paraphrases, and sometimes almost direct quotations from the Bible and Catholic catechism. In addition, all un-Christian viewpoints, such as not making peace with the enemies outside the tribe, found in Sword's remarks, are completely absent from Black Elk's account.

Clyde Holler continues the discussion. He calls attention to Black Elk's remark to Joseph Brown: that just as Christ is coming at the end of the world, so the White Buffalo Calf Woman comes with the Sacred Pipe. Holler understands this as an identification of the Pipe with Christ (1984:42). I believe this is a valid interpretation of Black Elk's symbolic thinking. Black Elk's explanation of the Sun Dance also brings out this same synthesis. Black Elk abandons the traditional purpose of individual vows "made in time of anxiety, usually on the warpath" (Densmore 1918:86, 88–91), for, instead, taking on the suffering of the people that they may live, a purpose which shows a Christian influence. But the Sun Dance symbols also acquire a Christian meaning. An armlet of rabbit skin represents humility "because he is quiet, soft and not self-asserting." Black Elk also removes most of the references to war and interprets the color black as representing ignorance and sin. And so Black Elk frees the Sun Dance from its association with the hunter warrior complex and gives it a new interpretation "in terms relevant to the radically changed conditions of reservation life," including the acceptance of Christianity. This is done in terms "commensurate with Christianity" (Holler 1984:44–48).

However, Holler's evaluation of Black Elk's relationship to Christianity needs examination. He places Black Elk in the Ecumenist I position and then states that he worked consciously to integrate the two traditions (1984:41). However, this is the Ecumenist II position, which Holler develops with such insight.

> The first is that it is typical of Black Elk's way of thinking and speaking to read back into his great vision an insight that could only have occurred to him after his years as a catechist. The same "reading back" characterizes Black Elk's entire account of the seven rites of the Lakota. Second, there is no hint of substitution in Black Elk's statement. Christ does not replace the pipe; both have co-equal validity. Third, and most obviously, Black Elk is saying to the Sioux, in what was to be his last written statement, that Indians should "pray with the pipe," that is, not abandon traditional religious practices for Christianity (42).

Black Elk reads back into his Lakota tradition the insights he acquired as a Catholic catechist. This is exactly what the early Christian converts from Judaism did with the Old Testament, making it a foreshadowing of Christ which reaches its fulfillment in Him (Steinmetz 1970). And so, Black Elk does the same, making Lakota religious tradition an "Old Testament" foreshadowing of Christ and reaching its fulfillment in Him. Secondly, Christ does not replace the Pipe since the Pipe becomes a cultural expression of Christ in becoming symbolically identified with Him. Third, the Lakota should not abandon their traditional religion for Christianity, but neither should they abandon their Christianity for their Lakota religion. Black Elk seems to be telling them privately to practice a Lakota Christian religion, since Lakota religion has acquired a Christian value. However, as a Catholic catechist he was unable to preach this publicly.

My first reason for putting Black Elk in the Ecumenist II position was primarily because of the mediating symbol of the Ghost Dance Messiah, recognized as Christ. It was Black Elk's unconscious which gave him the primary bridge between the two religious traditions from which his conscious activity flowed. My second reason is Black Elk's conscious integration of the two traditions, which DeMallie and Holler bring out. In answering Holler's comment: "But Steinmetz' Black Elk does not seem truly to be an example of the Ecumenist II position, since on Steinmetz' reading, as suggested by the recollections of Lame Goose, Black Elk is decidedly more Christian than traditional" (1984:41), I would like to suggest the following. I believe that Black Elk fluctuated between the two positions, being in the Ecumenist I position when talking to the priests and being in the Ecumenist II one in talking to Fools Crow and others privately. This fluctuation explains why different people see Black Elk in such different light.

Holler also states that "Black Elk's 'conversion' was not what is normally considered a conversion—the substitution of one religion for another" (1984:47). However, Black Elk had made a total commitment to Christ, as was evident from his life as a catechist. During a retreat for catechists, Father Sialm, S.J., writes: "On the third day of that retreat, Nick Black Elk came to me with this very worthy resolution: 'We catechists resolve never to commit a mortal sin'" (1923:78). Conversion to Christianity does not mean giving up a religious tradition but rather giving it a Christian meaning, which Holler has so convincingly shown above. Although Black Elk may start on the level of phenomenology, recognizing common and equal religious forms in both religions (Christ and the Pipe are coequal), the fact still remains that for him all Lakota religion is to be practiced in a Christian context, that is, in a way compatible with Christianity. In Black Elk's mind his interpretation of the Sun Dance, influenced by Christian tradition, is the fulfillment of his Lakota tradition. To equate conversion with the substitution of one religion for another is an inaccurate notion which does no justice to the deep psychological relationship a person has with his or her past. And we must recall Black Elk's Ghost Dance vision in which the Lakota Messiah became Christ.

This discovery of Christ in Lakota Religion would be worked out in greater detail by the Lakota who followed him. It has taken place primarily in their religious imagination. The Shoshones and Northern Utes have accomplished the same inculturation in their Sun Dances, but Jorgensen has prejudged it as "pseudo-Christian" (1972:21).

For Plenty Wolf the rawhide effigy of the man hanging from the Sun Dance tree represented the return of Christ. Dorsey states that the rawhide effigy of the man was a phallic symbol of fertility (1894: 457), and this an apt symbol of the return of Christ, which will be a source of new life. In Densmore's account, this same effigy indicates that the enemy was conquered by supernatural help (1918:188)—also an apt symbol, since in His return Christ overcomes universal evil. But Plenty Wolf discovers other meanings. The rawhide effigy of the buffalo is the Old Testament and the one of the man is the New Testament. We can recall Erikson's comment that the buffalo represents the old Lakota way of life. So Plenty Wolf's identification of the buffalo with the Old Testament is a way of expressing the belief that the traditional Lakota religion is a preparation for Christ in a way similar to the Old Testament for the Jews. For Plenty Wolf this was an intuition on a symbolic level and not an articulated understanding on a reflective level.

Powers calls this claim "religious imperialism," saying it takes "raw faith" to see the Sacred Pipe as a foreshadowing of Christ. However, Powers is unable to see that Plenty Wolf had this "raw faith," which enabled him to see that the Lakota religious tradition, like the Old Testament, was a preparation of Christ. And this is not an "analytical imposition," as Powers claims (1986:118–19). It goes beyond the recognition on the level of phenomenology of the common religious forms that actually exist in both religious symbols. This symbolic identification can only mean that the Lakota religious tradition reaches its perfection in Christ. If it doesn't have this meaning, what meaning does it have? Jorgensen and Clemmer have the same difficulty as Powers (1978:43). The time is long overdue for anthropologists to realize that they cannot understand the traditional religion of a Native American Christian without understanding his Christian tradition.

Plenty Wolf has yet another Christian interpretation: "the piercing of the flesh in the Sun Dance is a reminder of the piercing of Jesus. When a man pierces his flesh, he is doing it in remembrance of Christ." And, according to Plenty Wolf, the man who brought the Sun Dance from Montana to the Lakota said that "he was doing something like Noah did, bringing his people on a certain boat. We are going through the Sun Dance and we are reaching our destination just like Noah reached his."

Fools Crow invited me to participate in the 1971 Sun Dance so as to express his own Christian understanding of this ceremony. He also compared the Sun Dance tree to the Christian cross (Mailes 1978: 200). We can also recall Cherry Seed's telling Fools Crow that in accepting the Pipe he was going into a house with many strings attached to it. On later reflection, Fools Crow thought that this house, the sacred place of the Pipe, was the Catholic Church.

As we noted earlier, Red Cloud sang a Sun Dance song with the Pipe during the communion part of the Mass on the Sun Dance grounds. Plenty Wolf also prayed with the Pipe in the church at Slim Butte. Iron Rope told Pete Fast Horse in my presence: "I am glad this Father is interested in the Pipe. He can use this Pipe at Mass. . . . I would like to have Father use the Pipe when he prays at Mass. In a mysterious way God will give him many privileges. I know what Father asks in the Mass, I know it will come true. That's certain. So he should take up his Pipe without any hesitation." Pete Catches also defended my praying with the Pipe on the grounds that as a priest I was the equivalent of a "holy man" in the traditional Lakota sense. When he put me on the hill for a two-day Pipe fast in 1974, he told me that some would criticize him for this but that this was one of the great honors of his life. Kills Ree, a yuwipi man, insisted that I pray with the Pipe at the burial of his grandson. I was really overwhelmed when I discovered that this Pipe had been in the Chips family for several generations.

Still other examples of Lakota Christian inculturation can be given. Edgar Red Cloud discovered a profound Christian meaning in Mother Earth, saying that "when the Indians knew Mother Earth, they knew the Blessed Virgin Mary but they did not know her by name." He also stated that the Woman who brought the Pipe is the Blessed Virgin Mary who brought Christ, an identification which another Lakota made to Kemnitzer (n.d.). Two Bulls tells how his grandfather translated the obligation of a Lakota dream into Christian terms: "He dreamt of the thunder. But he was a Christian man. So whenever it thundered, he took out his Bible and read it to fulfill his dream. Catches shares his own experience in saying that he prayed with his Pipe in memory of his vision "just as the priest changes bread and wine into the Body of Blood of Christ in memory of the Last Supper."

Finally, Benjamin Black Elk told me that during most of his life he was in doubt about the relation between the Pipe and Christ. When he believed in the Pipe, was he betraying himself as a Christian? But, now that he saw that the Pipe and Christ were really one, his conscience's doubts of many years were ended and he had a deep spiritual peace in his soul. And that night the vision of the Pipe leading the Lakota to Christ, which we shared in his log cabin, made a deep impression on both of us.

These Lakota courageously discovered the presence of Christ in their Lakota religious tradition at a time when most of the missionaries were condemning it as un-Christian. As Fools Crow told me: "I never talked about the Pipe to a Catholic priest in the early days, but I brought the two religions together on my own." It was the Lakota medicine men and not the Christian missionaries who had the insight, even though on a symbolic level, that the traditional Lakota religion was pre-Christian. I have the humility to admit with Powers that the medicine men were impressed that I had "finally seen the light" (1977:116). And I have the deepest respect for the Lakota holy men who in their own way professed that the meaning of the Pipe in its maturity is Christ. How far these few have come since the first intimation of Christ which Black Elk had in the Ghost Dance Messiah vision.

The Ecumenist I Group

The Ecumenist I group consists of those Lakota Christians who have both Lakota and Christian identities, or a split identity. Their Lakota identity is expressed through the traditional Pipe, and their Christian one through the Bible as a white value in the traditional Christian Church. Although their primary identity may be Lakota, it does not follow that their Christian one is superficial, as has so often been claimed. The ambivalence towards Lakota spirits, life after death, and other religious symbols show this viewpoint to be an oversimplification. As Powers states, they move back and forth situationally between the Lakota and Christian ends of the continuum. Each religion fulfills their needs in particular circumstances and times. There seems to be a certain dissatisfaction with both religious traditions, so that they see complementary values in both—as, for example, seeking healing through a yuwipi ceremony and seeking counseling in personal problems from the Christian minister or priest.

But there is a continuum within their Christian identity. This identity can be considered a continuum between the Ecumenist II position on one end and a minimal participation in the Christian churches on the other. Members of this group move towards the Ecumenist II end by discovering common religious forms in both the Lakota and the Christian symbols on the level of phenomenology. These common forms include the concept of power, of Messiah, of mediator, and of spiritual healing. They mediate between the two religious traditions through a transfer of emotional energy which happens, for example, when the same sense of power is felt in both the Lakota and Christian symbols. I believe that this mediation sometimes allows their Christian tradition to form a continuity with the Lakota one on both conscious and unconscious levels so that the Lakota avoids the symbolic sickness that Powers describes (1977:206).

This mediation can be achieved even though it is an imperfect stage of the Ecumenist II position. The Lakota in the Ecumenist I position recognizes common forms in both religions but not their Lakota religion as explicitly Christian. It is the difference between the beliefs of Eagle Feather and Black Elk. Eagle Feather, in saying "the Pipe is our Christ," saw the religious form of saviour in both the Lakota and Christian. Black Elk made his Lakota religion explicitly Christian in saying this Lakota "wanekia is the Son of the Great Spirit Himself." It is the comparison of form on the level of phenomenology as compared to inculturation. But if the recognition of common religious forms is sufficiently deep, then the Ecumenist I position achieves some stability.

If, on the other hand, the awareness of common religious forms in both the Lakota and the Christian tradition is not present, then there is usually a movement towards the other end of the continuum within the Christian identity, that is toward minimal participation in the traditional churches with the indifference it involves. In other words, a split personal identity can result in an unstable psychological state. For some Lakota at this end of the continuum, the American Indian Movement gave them the opportunity to discover their latent Lakota identity. It is very unlikely for a person in the Ecumenist II group to move into another one. This we observed in the opposition of the medicine men to the anti-Christian attitude of AIM despite their sympathy towards its social and political goals.

Beyond doubt, the Ecumenist I group contains the majority of the Lakota people. Thus, the analysis of this group offers a contribution to the theory of religious acculturation by giving new insights into the shifting patterns of religious affiliations among the Oglala Lakota.

The Native American Church, Cross Fire Fireplace

The importance of the Native American church among the Oglala Lakota to the theory of religious acculturation resides particularly in its intimate connection with both the Bible and the Pipe. LaBarre lists several pages of Christian elements in Peyote and yet comes to the conclusion "that the layer of Christianity on peyotism is very thin and superficial indeed" (1975:166). He further states that "the Mission of El Santo Nombre de Jesus Peyotes [venerated in the region of Villa Union in Coah, Mexico since 1690] is so called merely from the abundance of the plant thereabouts" (162). However, what LaBarre is apparently unaware of is that a prayer to this Jesus of Peyote has the official approbation of a Catholic bishop, His Excellency Dr. Don Luis Guizar Barragan, and was distributed on printed holy cards (one is in the possession of Emerson Spider). The local bishop, at least, took the devotion seriously. LaBarre also mentions that the "Delaware followers of Wilson call the corn husk cigarette the 'pipe of Jesus'" (163). This designation is highly significant since, as we shall see, it integrates the same three religious traditions which the Lakota Half Moon members do. (I think LaBarre lacks an appreciation of symbolic signification.) Finally, Mooney wrote back in 1892:

"It may be proper to state that many of the mescal [Peyote] eaters wear crucifixes, which they regard as sacred emblems of the rite, the cross representing the cross of scented leaves upon which the consecrated mescal rests during the ceremony, while the Christ is the mescal goddess" (1892:65). Stewart's comment is relevant here: "I believe Peyotism was strongly influenced from Mexico when it was first introduced into the United States and that a number of Christian elements were already present when the fully established Peyote ritual was first observed by Mooney in 1892" (1977:931). But Opler, too, had a bias similar to LaBarre's: "Indeed, far from becoming a weakened and Christianized version of native beliefs, the Mescalero Apache acceptance of peyote resulted instead in an intensification of the aboriginal religious values and concepts at many points" (1936:144). He implies that in this case a Christian version must be a weakened one and that the intensification of aboriginal values is incompatible with Christianity. We will see just how wrong these assumptions are, at least with the Oglala Lakota.

The Cross Fire fireplace among the Oglala Lakota leaves no doubt of the strong Christian identity of Peyote. Emerson Spider clearly states that when he believes in Christ and reads the Bible, he is not a white man but a 100 percent Indian. And, at the State Convention in the summer of 1978, he told the members that neither the Cross Fire nor the Half Moon fireplaces are of any value unless they lead to Christ. The Bible has replaced the ceremonial cigarette in practice, even though Spider urges his members to respect the Half Moon tradition and if they attend a Half Moon meeting, they must do it their way and take part in the ceremonial smoke. Baptism is necessary to be a member of the Cross Fire. The Bible is always on the altar beneath the chief Peyote. The midnight water talk is always from the Bible. Cross Fire ministers are ordained. A member has even been appointed to the position of Bible teacher. Gospel singing has been introduced into some Peyote meetings. Spider's intense evangelical spirit is very obvious from an interview he had with Raymond DeMallie in August of 1982. (Spider 1987:20, 189–209). Some of the members are born-again Christians (197). As a fifteen-year-old boy, Spider took Peyote and was healed by Christ (198). And so they don't give large quantities of medicine as they did in the old days, since they are now relying on the healing of Jesus Christ (205). These are just a few of Spider's statements indicating a strong Christian identity.

Recently the Christian basis of the church has been made even more explicit. In October of 1979, Emerson Spider, Sr., Rev. William Richards, Rene Mills, Wilson Crow, and Mrs. Verolo Spider-Mills filed Articles of Incorporation for the Native American Church of Jesus Christ. Article III contains the purpose: "To promulgate the Christian Doctrine set forth by the scriptures of the HOLY BIBLE. To proclaim the teachings of JESUS CHRIST in an Indian way of worship to all AMERICAN INDIANS who may reside in the STATE OF SOUTH DAKOTA and within the UNITED STATES OF AMERICA. Moreover, to specifically promulgate the teaching of JESUS CHRIST to the AMERICAN INDIANS who customarily utilize the GOD GIVEN HERB (PEYOTE) in their Indian ways of worship of almighty GOD." This is perhaps the first Native American Church charter that explicitly mentions Peyote and has the Name of Jesus Christ in its official charter. Although the Cross Fire fireplace is not mentioned in the Articles of Incorporation, the incorporators presently intend to make this the exclusive fireplace in the bylaws when they are written. Rene Mills considers the Half Moon fireplace as an imperfect expression of Christ, as the Old Testament is.

The Native American Church, Cross Fire, is one alternative to a Lakota Christian church. The identity that is in consciousness most frequently is the Lakota one rather than the pan-Indian one. In fact, the Cross Fire has a weak pan-Indian identity on a national American level. They have obtained only state charters. During the summer of 1978, a proposal was made to sponsor a national convention on the Pine Ridge Reservation. The State Chairman showed no interest on the grounds that the national people have never helped the Native American Church in South Dakota. The Cross Fire represents a Lakota Christian identity that neither rejects traditional Lakota religious symbols as the Body of Christ Independent Church nor inculturates them as the Ecumenist II. Instead, there is the same inculturation of Christ in the Peyote among them as the Ecumenist II have achieved in the Pipe. In Spider's viewpoint, Christ is the real center of the Native American Church. Certainly, for the Cross Fire fireplace of the Native American Church among the Oglala Lakota, Christianity is no thin and superficial layer over peyotism.

The Native American Church, Half Moon Fireplace

The Half Moon fireplace represents a Lakota Christian identity which is expressed through three religious traditions. The Half Moon has a Lakota identity because it integrates traditional Lakota religious symbols, especially the Pipe, into their ceremonies. The old man Red Bear always prayed with the Pipe at his meetings. The practice was subsequently followed by Hawkins, Gap, and on occasion by Red Bear's great-grandson, Solomon. In addition, the Lakota word *Cannunpa* ("Pipe") is used for the ceremonial cigarette, creating a strong awareness of the cigarette standing for the Pipe. The symbol of the Pipe is as closely associated with the Half Moon as the Bible is with the Cross Fire, even though the actual Pipe is rarely brought into a Peyote meeting. In the Half Moon fireplace there is a whole range of traditional symbols: the roadman goes outside to pray in the four directions; there are four smokes and four water calls; sage is used to rub oneself with as protection against the evil spirits. Many members move back and forth between traditional Lakota ceremonies and Peyote meetings according to what best fulfills their needs at the time.

The Half Moon fireplace also has a strong Christian identity, even though the Bible is not actually present during the meeting. The Name of Jesus is included in both song and prayer. But the depth of feeling with which John Weasel Bear talked about the Sacred Heart of Jesus and Mary beneath the cross during a Peyote meeting at the midnight water call brings out more than any comments the depth of Christian commitment. The following prayer excerpt is from a Mother's Day meeting.

"This evening we have the heart [the ash formation in the fireplace], the Sacred Heart of Jesus. This heart means a lot of things to this religion, to the Native American Church. It has a lot of concern in there. Coming to Mother's Day. Even the Lord when He was crucified, He looked down upon His mother. His mother was standing below Him there. He didn't say anything to her. All He could do was to shed tears; He cried. That's all He could do. So His mother was standing below and looking up at Him. There was nothing she could do. So the Lord gave Himself for the people that are here on this earth. Not only across the ocean but over here too, for the Indian people.

He gave His life for you. The Great Spirit so loved the world that He died for you. From that time on, that is the way this Sacred Heart of Jesus came about. If any person believes in God, the Great Spirit, He said thou shall love thy neighbor as thyself. That's what the teaching of the Native American Church is."

Half Moon members do not have the same intense evangelical spirit as some of the Cross Fire ones, but they do have a definite Christian identity today, admitting an historical development.

The Half Moon fireplace is a remarkable example of religious acculturation in that it integrates the three religious traditions of Pipe, Bible, and Peyote. (A comparative study with other reservations would be of great value to determine how unique the Native American Church among the Oglala Lakota may be.) The Half Moon members have a greater sense of pan-Indian identity than the Cross Fire, as is reflected in their obtaining a National Charter from Oklahoma and renewing it three times. And yet, at the same time, they have a stronger Lakota identity. That both the pan-Indian and Lakota identities are stronger than the Cross Fire's is a remarkable phenomenon, showing that they are compatible. Finally, there is an inculturation of both the traditional Lakota and Christian symbols in the Peyote ceremonies. The celebration of this inculturation took place in the Peyote meeting described earlier, in which the Papal Blessing, the Pipe, and the Peyote were present on the Half Moon altar.

CONCLUSIONS

We are able now to make some concluding observations from the model of religious identity.

First, there are mutual influences between Pipe, Bible, and Peyote in the process of religious acculturation. When some Lakota identify the Calf Pipe Woman who brought the Pipe with the Blessed Virgin Mary who brought Christ, both religious traditions acquire a new meaning. Through their association with each other, both symbols are understood in a new light. We should not overlook the emotional associations which may be involved.

Secondly, the Pipe and Peyote both become mediating symbols. The Ecumenist II's understanding of the Pipe makes it a mediating symbol between the traditional Lakota and Christian religions. Spider's understanding of Peyote as leading to Christ makes it, also, a mediating symbol between those two traditions. The Half Moon members' perception of the ceremonial cigarette as a substitute for the Pipe makes smoking the cigarette a mediating symbol between the Native American Church and traditional Lakota Religion.

Third, the same attitude towards one of the religious symbols can result in a different practice. The American Indian Movement, considering the Bible as a white man's value, rejects it for "pure Lakota Religion." Those who take the Ecumenist I position have the same attitude towards the Bible but consider it an alternative to Lakota religion under certain circumstances.

Fourth, an attitude towards a religious symbol can be distinguished by whether a symbol is for oneself or others. Both Ecumenist I Lakota and Native American Church Cross Fire members perceive the Pipe as an alternate to the Bible. But the Ecumenist I persons consider this as an actual choice and participate in traditional ceremonies, while Cross Fire members do not (while nevertheless respecting those who do).

Fifth, there is both continuity and discontinuity between the Pipe and the Bible. We saw how the rawhide effigy of the man on the Sun Dance tree perceived both as a fertility symbol and as the enemy overcome by supernatural means in the past showed both continuity and discontinuity with Plenty Wolf's perception of it as a symbol of the return of Christ.

Sixth, Pipe, Bible, and Peyote represent dynamic states, not static ones. There are alternating states of consciousness between pan-Indian and Lakota identities. There are shifting relationships which result from an Ecumenist I Lakota moving back and forth on the continuum between traditional Lakota and traditional Christian religions as well as on the continuum between Ecumenist II and superficial Christianity within his Christian identity. There are shifting relationships of the Half Moon members, moving back and forth between traditional Lakota ceremonies and Peyote meetings. Finally, a Lakota may embrace several positions at the same time in regard to different aspects of his beliefs. He may be in the Ecumenist II position in his basic understanding of the Pipe and move to the Ecumenist I position in the practice of yuwipi. All the various continuums discussed above are simply ways of conceptualizing the various alternating states of religious experience. Alternations between the conscious and the unconscious would add yet another dimension to the model.

This by no means exhausts the opportunities for future field studies in religious identity, but it does indicate a method of approach in the complex shifting religious patterns, both within each religious group and between them, which are a part of the Oglala Lakota identity.

Finally, it seems that the above evidence establishes an important conclusion. One cannot understand the traditional religion of a Native American Christian without understanding his or her Christian religion. And the reverse is true. One cannot understand the Christian religion of this same person without understanding the traditional religion. I think both the missionary and the anthropologist have misunderstood the religious situation of the Native Americans. The Native Americans did not embrace a Christianity divorced from their traditional religions, as the missionary assumed, nor did they practice a traditional religion unaffected by their Christianity, as the anthropologist assumed. And whether a religion is practiced wholeheartedly or superficially depends upon the person. Black Elk practiced his Lakota religion with complete dedication, and he did the same with his Christian religion. And in some instances the Native American who is superficial in Christian religion is also superficial in the traditional religion.

EPILOGUE

Religious acculturation among the Oglala Lakota on the Pine Ridge Reservation can be compared to a tapestry woven from the rich religious experience of Pipe, Bible, and Peyote. It is impossible to unravel the threads of contemporary Oglala Lakota religion. Each religious group has contributed. The American Indian Movement helped young Lakota get in touch with the religious symbols deep in their psyches, through a revival of traditional Lakota Religion. The Body of Christ Church is a witness of conversion and commitment to Christ among the Lakota. The Native American Church offers the opportunity of another approach to religious experience in harmony with Lakota identity. Ecumenist I and Ecumenist II add a new Christian dimension to traditional Lakota religion, making up for some of its deficiencies and in turn being enriched by it. Pipe, Bible, and Peyote are all part of the search for a new religious identity.

Densmore had already noticed this acculturation process when she observed the "repent, repent" exhortation of the Sun Dance intercessor. Sword accepted the same religious form of power in both the Lakota Wakantanka and the white man's God. Black Elk recognized the Ghost Dance Messiah as the Lakota Christ. Ecumenist II Lakota recognized the presence of Christ in their religious symbols. Lakota religion has enriched the Christian churches with its own living symbols, and the Christian churches, in turn, have given Lakota religion an intimacy found in a personal relationship with Jesus Christ, the Son of the Great Spirit. Is it possible, perhaps, that the Lakota Christ of Black Elk's Messiah vision becoming fully conscious in a newly revived Lakota Christian Religion may be the flowering tree in the center of the nation's hoop? (DeMallie 1984:240, 259).

APPENDICES

APPENDIX A

The Homily at the Funeral of Benjamin Black Elk

This homily is included because of its importance in helping us understand those parts of the Black Elk tradition which have been neglected. It is a contribution to the well-balanced view which Raymond DeMallie developed in The Sixth Grandfather.

We come here today as a faith community to celebrate the eternal life of Benjamin Black Elk. We know his soul lives on and enters into the spirit world. Benjamin came from a great tradition. He had a father who was very important in the life of the Oglala Lakota. His father, Nicholas Black Elk, was perhaps the greatest Lakota mystic in the history of the Lakota people. He was the St. John of the Cross of the Oglala Lakota people. And from his vision he derived from God a gift of prophecy and a gift of healing which were very great. In these visions as a Lakota holy man the seeds of Christ were planted. He not only was converted to the Catholic Church but he was the greatest Catholic catechist on the reservation. Probably no man is more responsible for the planting of the Catholic Church at Manderson than Nicholas Black Elk. Perhaps this is the part of his life that is not well enough known. I can remember Ben telling me that his was the chapter in *Black Elk Speaks* that is not yet written. It is wonderful that this book, a great gift to the Indian people and to mankind, reveals to us the visions of this holy man. Yet Ben said that this book was incomplete, that someday he would have to write the last chapter, of his father as a Catholic catechist establishing the church here in Manderson. And he said that this would be the greatest and most important chapter of his father's life. And so it is fitting then that Ben had this spiritual training from his father, a training in two religious traditions. It would be a preparation then for a very unusual life.

Many years ago now, Ben Black Elk rode through the Black Hills seeking the spirit of his son, Benjamin Jr., who had passed into the other world. And it was this search that eventually led to his involvement at Mount Rushmore. And I think here we have an example of a proud Indian who literally greeted millions of people for a quarter of a century. I remember seeing him being so wonderful and being so open with small children. He had a winning way with the little children. And I would reflect on the story in the Gospel, of Christ calling the little children to Himself and He would not have them turned away. Ben Black Elk won the hearts of the American people. He certainly was an ambassador of good will. He captured the hearts of America.

But I think there is a much more important side of Ben Black Elk. There is his religious side. I can remember talking to him in his home about his religious searching, about his seeking to understand his own religious traditions, seeking to understand more deeply the life experience of his father as interpreted to the world through *Black Elk Speaks* and the *Sacred Pipe*. He was not satisfied with the understanding he had. He was seeking for a deeper and deeper understanding. Ben Black Elk was also a very strong Catholic. Ben, along with all mankind, with all of us, sinned and failed against almighty God. From my own personal experience I know he had a deep faith in the sacrament of confession. He knew there was a sacred power in the absolution of the priest. He knew he had a religious ceremony of purification to which he could go whenever it was needed. I saw Ben Black Elk receive this sacrament with great sincerity, with great faith and with great feeling.

This particular night we were talking together about the relationship of the vision of his father, of the Lakota religion, and his Catholic faith. We talked about this because both of these traditions meant very much to him. And we began to talk about the fact that there was no conflict between the two. And we talked about how the Sacred Pipe could lead a person to Christ and how the Sacred Pipe was a foreshadowing of Christ in His great office of mediator, of bringing man back to the Great Spirit. We talked, then, of how Christ fulfilled the traditions of the Sacred Pipe and how Christ is the living and eternal Pipe. And then Ben made a very startling confession to me. He said that through most of his life there was a conflict between these two traditions. He did have doubts of conscience. When he lectured on the Sacred Pipe and had a belief in the Sacred Pipe, was he betraying himself as a Christian? He said that now that he sees that the Sacred Pipe and Christ really are one, that they fulfill each other, the doubts of conscience of many years have ended. Now he had real spiritual peace in his soul. And this shared vision of the Sacred Pipe leading the Lakota people to Christ as the Living and Eternal Pipe made a deep impression on both of us. And this is what I would like to call the vision of Benjamin Black Elk.

In a way this vision was much more powerful and much more needed than even the visions of his father, Nicholas Black Elk. I think it is a vision that it would be well for all of us, as we look up now to the traditions of our fathers, to take to heart, a vision that we could pray over and explore. It is Christ, the God man, then, that gathers from the four directions the entire universe and carries it back to the Great Spirit in a way that fulfills the Sacred Pipe and does not destroy it. I think that this acceptance of Christ was a very important thing in the life of Benjamin Black Elk. It will be this vision that is going to help as we bring a living culture to the Oglala Lakota people today. I believe this vision is an important foundation of two cultures that are beginning to come to life on this reservation.

And so now we gather together to celebrate the eternal life of this great man. A man who holds out to us the hope of a better life, the hope of a more spiritual life.

Reading from the prophet Isaiah, what a wonderful picture it is, life in heaven. On this mountain the Lord of hosts will provide to all peoples; He will prepare a banquet, a banquet in which we will have a great deal of joy. For God will wipe away the tears of all peoples. He will take away our shame and our reproach. And so this is the heavenly banquet to which Benjamin has been called. And this is the heavenly banquet in which all of us someday will share. This is the heavenly banquet of which the Mass is but the sign or foreshadowing. We gather at the Eucharistic meal which will lead someday to the heavenly banquet to which Ben Black Elk has been called. And it is very evident in the early Church that the Christians were called to accept Jesus Christ as their Savior and Lord and to receive His power. And with this they were anointed with the Holy Spirit and with power. This is what Nicholas Black Elk certainly had, power as a holy man and power as a Catholic catechist. I think this is what Benjamin inherited, an influence and a power with people, one in which his memory and name will go on for a very long time.

Ben was very much impressed with the ceremony of the Sacred Pipe at the graveside which he saw performed for his friends. In this ceremony Ben made this great act of faith, that Christ is the Resurrection and the Life. Any man that believes in me, he will not die forever, he will not die spiritually. If he believes in Me, the Resurrection and the Life, his life goes on. And our Lord asked Benjamin the very same question He asked Martha: "Do you believe this?" And, along with Martha, Ben said "Yes, Lord, I believe You are the Messiah, the one who is to come and save the world." And then in that cabin that night, when he could see that Christ is the Living and Eternal Pipe, this act of faith, this vision, brought both of his religious traditions together. And I feel deep in my heart that this is the greatest achievement of Benjamin Black Elk. This is the crown of his spiritual life, of his spiritual groping. This vision in which we are all welcome to share in, this is his heritage to the Oglala Lakota.

And so we open our hearts and we turn now to the relatives, to those close and near to him, to those who will miss him so much, to the countless people who have such a deep love and affection for Ben Black Elk. We turn to them and we ask all these people to open up their hearts to the Holy Spirit, to let the spirit of Christ come in with peace, with understanding, with acceptance of God's will, to believe that God is a loving Father, that he does direct the lives of each one of us, including the life of Ben, according to His best plan to lead us to salvation. We open our hearts up to the hope for the resurrection. We open our hearts up to the peace of Christ, the same peace that Ben had that night in his cabin. Let the Holy Spirit come into our lives. May the blessing of almighty God descend upon each and everyone of us. Amen.

APPENDIX B

Homily at the Funeral of George Plenty Wolf

This homily is included as a tribute to a medicine man who bridged two religious worlds, at times in opposition to the Catholic Church which he so dearly loved. It is a contribution to understanding the developing relationship between the Christian Church and the Lakota people.

I chose to wear red vestments this morning because red is the sacred color of power. And we are celebrating this morning the life of a man who experienced power. He knew what power was, not only the power of the Sacred Pipe but also the power of Jesus Christ. He knew both powers in his life. And he really believed in both powers. And so we celebrate the ceremony with red vestments, with the sacred color of power.

The first time I laid the Sacred Pipe on a coffin was at the funeral of Rex Long Visitor at Slim Butte. I don't do that often. I feel a man has to really be worthy for me to lay the Sacred Pipe on his coffin. And I felt very strongly that this was the case with George. At that funeral of Rex Long Visitor about eleven years ago, George was there. And I remember George praying with the Sacred Pipe before the dinner, praying and blessing the food. And so George was with me since that very first day. We were very close because of this.

George Plenty Wolf was a deeply spiritual man. God called him in his early days to the work of a catechist at Manderson and around Holy Rosary. And then He called him to another work. God called George up to the hill to fast with the Pipe and to acquire a vision. And through this vision to acquire a power through one of God's greatest gifts, the Sacred Pipe. And George really believed in the Sacred Pipe. He believed there was power there and that his prayers would be answered. George also believed in Jesus Christ. I remember George walking into Pine Ridge all the way from the Red Cloud community as an old man, walking to attend Mass on Sunday. I remember giving him Holy Communion. And he had a great and a deep faith in the death and resurrection of Jesus Christ. And he also had a great faith that there was power in the sacraments containing the Presence of Christ. The first day he was in the hospital, about two weeks before his death, I anointed him with the anointing of the sick and I brought him Holy Communion and he blessed himself very reverently with great devotion. I could really see in his face, in his eyes, that he really believed in the sacraments, in Jesus Christ's Body.

I think George Plenty Wolf was an important man for the Lakota people. He was a man who walked in the traditional way, a man who prayed for people and carried the burdens of people because he was a "Pipe man." Yet he was also a man who recognized that the Sacred Pipe had a place in the Christian Church. George accepted my praying with the Sacred Pipe. And this meant something very much to me. I was very deeply grateful, since he was a medicine man and a "Pipe man." But it was something much more than simply personal. I feel that what George was doing was accepting the Pipe into the Christian Church. And I think that this is a very important thing he did in his life. And this is going to become more and more important now as the Lakota people go back to their roots and tradition. Here was the vision of a man who saw the Sacred Pipe as one of God's great gifts that should be brought to the feet of Jesus Christ and laid there since Jesus Christ is the Son of God. And I really believe in my heart that this is a most important vision and this is one of the greatest things George ever did in his life and to become more important as the years go on.

I feel that perhaps the life of George can be summarized in kind of a double vision. George was the man who was looking towards the hill. On the hill he saw a man with the Sacred Pipe fasting and receiving a vision and as he looked, he kept on looking up on that hill and that man with the Sacred Pipe changed into Jesus Christ hanging on the cross. This is the double image I feel summarized his life more than anything else.

What kind of man was George Plenty Wolf? He was a very kind man, a very gentle man. Someone who knew George for a long time told me that he never saw George angry. And this has been my own experience. He was a very humble man. He knew where his power came from. His powers came from the Great Spirit. He was simply the instrument of God. And George knew his limitations. I remember very clearly when one of his grandchildren had an epileptic fit, he told the people that he did not have the power to heal this, that she should be taken up to the hospital and that the priest should be called, that the priest should anoint her with the sacrament of healing. This is really genuine humility before Almighty God. I think George was a very patient man.

George carried the burdens of many people. Many people came to him for prayers. Carrying the Sacred Pipe meant he had to respond to these requests. Throughout his life George carried the burdens of many people. George healed people. There is no doubt in my mind that when the spirit of George left this world there were countless spirits whom he helped in this life waiting to receive him. What a reception that must have been. The spirits of all these people through all those years waiting now to receive the spirit of George.

I think George was a very understanding man. He had a calling from God and had a vision that made him walk the path of the Sacred Pipe, and he had a great love of Jesus Christ. And yet there were times that he was misunderstood, misunderstood by the Church he loved so much. And yet George had the patience and the understanding to accept this and to work in his own life to bring the two traditions together. I feel that this is very remarkable. And so we celebrate today the eternal life of a truly remarkable man. We celebrate the eternal life of one the people are going to miss, the community, the Lakota nation.

The Lord looked down and the Lord said: "The life of George is now completed. His work is finished. The spiritual work I gave George to do is now accomplished, and I will call George back to Myself." And, in words of Isaiah, on this mountain God will remove the mourning veil; on this mountain the Lord of hosts will provide for all people; on this mountain He will destroy death forever. The mountain is a holy, a sacred place. And on the hill George came into very close contact with God, his Father. And it is on this mountain that God will wipe away the tears from our faces. And we are going to say: "Behold our God to Whom we are going to look to save us." And this is done according to the words of Isaiah on the holy mountain.

And, in the Acts of the Apostles, St. Peter said: "I know it is true now that God is not going to show partiality, that God sent His Son, Jesus Christ, for all peoples and for all nations to proclaim the good news of peace and to lead people to accept that Jesus Christ is Lord." Jesus Christ is Lord of all nations, all peoples, of all continents. Jesus Christ is Lord of the Lakota People. And this is the great act of faith that George Plenty Wolf made. And then St. Peter continues, and he tells the way that in the baptism of John God anointed Christ with the Holy Spirit and power. And I thought that this is George Plenty Wolf. He too was anointed with the Holy Spirit and with power. And how Christ went around doing good works and healing all who were in the grip of the devil. I really feel that this is a description of the life of George in his work of prayer and in his work of being a man who carried the Sacred Pipe.

They finally killed Christ, hanging Him on a tree, only to have God raise Him up on the third day. And so we come to this great mystery of the death and resurrection of Christ. It is a mystery that doesn't contradict the mystery of the Sacred Pipe. But it brings us deeper into the mystery of the Great Spirit. He sent not only His great gift, the Sacred Pipe, to the Lakota People, but He sent His own Son, Jesus Christ also. In the Gospel, Christ said: "Whoever eats my flesh and drinks my blood will have everlasting life." He told the people that their fathers ate the manna in the desert when they were coming out of Egypt and died. But whoever eats His flesh will live forever. We know with certitude that these words apply to George Plenty Wolf. Our Lord speaks these words to him.

Midakuase. For the sake of my relatives. This is what George said so often as he concluded his ceremonies with the Sacred Pipe. And this is the way we conclude our thoughts, for the sake of our relatives. We offer up the Sacrifice of the Mass for the spirit of George praying for all the relatives. We ask God to bless his children and his grandchildren, to bless all those who are related to him, all those who are close to him, to pour the Holy Spirit into their hearts, to give them strength and courage, to bless them with the vision of the death and resurrection of Christ, that we are all living this great mystery and with the assurance that God has called George back to Himself, to eternal happiness. May the Holy Spirit be poured into their hearts with His peace and His joy, His consolation and hope and love. That the Holy Spirit may be with them now at this time.

NOTES

INTRODUCTION

1. More detailed information can be obtained from P. Beckwith (1886), DeLand (1904/1906), William Forbes (1894), Hayden (1863), Hyde (1937, 1956), Mekeel (1943), Robinson (1904), and Yarrow (1882).
2. Anyone wishing to pursue further the relationship between Eliade and Jung should also consult Mac Linscott Ricketts. (1970:221–34).
3. There is a growing literature on Red Power and Indian activism, including Burnette (1974), and Steiner (1969).
4. The Native Americans are using the term *ecumenism* in an annual pan-Indian Ecumenical Conference which unites Native American spiritual leaders of the United States and Canada from all religious faiths, indigenous and Christian.

CHAPTER ONE

1. John Smith has an excellent historical background (1967) and indicates its contemporary effect, including its use in the Catholic Church (1970). Wilbur Reigert interviewed one of its previous keepers, Martha Bad Warrior, on its history (1975:71–94).
2. However, the bundle was opened for Reigert, a Chippewa Indian, in 1936 (1975:73) and for an anthropologist, Sidney Thomas, in 1941. Sidney J. Thomas gives a detailed description of the bundle contents, including the Pipe regarded as the Calf Pipe (1941); Smith describes a related ceremony for the preparation of the offering cloths (1964).
3. Kenneth Philip has a complete evaluation of Collier's relation to the American Indian (1977).
4. Mails had additional information on Fools Crow (1979:49–53).
5. Fletcher (1882), Schwatka (1890) and Webb (MS. 1894) also describe the Sun Dance during the 1880s.
6. A memorial give-away is usually associated with the memorial feast

conducted one year after a person's death. At that time a meal is prepared for relatives and friends. After the meal, many possessions are given away to honor the deceased person. These gifts include star quilts and dancing shawls, which relatives make during the course of the year, and suitcases, dinnerware, and other practical items bought at stores. During the Sun Dance, only the giving away of possessions takes place.

7. The entire homily is found in Appendix A.
8. William Stolzman, S.J., has excellent original ethnographic material on the spirits which supplements the material obtained from the Lakota here (1986:104–15).
9. Kemnitzer (1976:261–80) and Powers (1982) both have excellent treatments of yuwipi as a modern healing ceremony among the Lakota.
10. A winter count is the recording of historical events by means of pictures painted on a buffalo hide. One of the most important Sioux winter counts is the one recorded by Baptiste Good in the first part of last century. For a complete description consult Mallery (1893: 287–328).
11. Frederick Streng discusses the sacred/profane dichotomy in some detail (1980 16:122–26).
12. The coup stick was used by a warrior to touch the enemy, either dead or alive. To touch an alive enemy and escape brought even more honor than touching the dead body. The expression "counting coup" developed from this practice.
13. Christoph von Fürer-Haimendorf in a cross-cultural study brings out just how diverse this concept can be (1974).

CHAPTER TWO

1. Blue Bird told Stewart (n.d.) that he went to Oklahoma in 1902. This confirms the statement of Bernard Red Cloud.
2. This corrects the diffusion charts of Shonle, LaBarre, Driver, and Massey referred to above.
3. The sponsor is the person responsible for the meeting taking place and for its purpose. The water woman is the person who brings in the ceremonial water and blesses it at the conclusion of the meeting.
4. It is reminiscent of the Shaking Tent rite among the Algonquian and Blackfoot.

CHAPTER FOUR

1. For an understanding of the Pipe among all the North American tribes, see Steinmetz 1984:27–80.
2. Although Kemnitzer reported a frequent use of Lakota in a 1966 revival meeting at Wolf Creek (personal notes), the service I attended in the summer of 1978 was entirely in English.

BIBLIOGRAPHY

Aberle, David F.
1966 *The Peyote Religion among the Navaho.* Chicago: Aldine.

Albers, Patricia, and Seymour Parker
1971 The Plains Vision Experience: A Study of Power and Privilege. *Southwestern Journal of Anthropology* 27:203–33.

Allen, Douglas
1978 *Structure and Creativity in Religious Hermeneutics in Mircea Eliade's Phenomenology and New Directions.* The Hague: Mouton.

Altizer, Thomas J.
1975 *Mircea Eliade and the Dialectic of the Sacred.* Westport, Conn.: Greenwood.

Amiotte, Arthur
1976 Eagles Fly Over. *Parabola* 1, no. 3: 28–41.

Beckwith, Martha Warren
1930 Mythology of the Oglala Dakota. *Journal of American Folklore* 43: 339–442.

Beckwith, P.
1886 Notes on Customs of the Dakotahs. *Smithsonian Institution, Annual Reports of the Board of Regents:* 245–57.

Benedict, Ruth F.
1922 Visions in Plains Culture. *American Anthropologist* 24:2–23.
1923 *The Concept of the Guardian Spirit in North America.* Memoirs of the American Anthropological Association, no. 29.
1936 Configurations of Culture. *American Anthropologist* 34:1–27.

Bennett, J. W., ed.
1975 The New Ethnicity: Perspectives from Ethnology. *1973 Proceedings of the American Ethnological Society.* St. Paul: West.

Berndt, R. M.
1962 *An Adjustment Movement in Arnhem Land, North Territory of Australia.* Paris and The Hague: Mouton.

Blish, Helen
1926 Ethical Conceptions of the Oglala Dakota. *University of Nebraska Studies* 26:1–47.
1934 The Ceremony of the Sacred Bow of the Oglala Dakota. *American Anthropologist* 36:180–87.
Blumensohn, Jules
1933 The Fast among North American Indians. *American Anthropologist* 35:451–69.
Brown, Joseph Epes
1953 *The Sacred Pipe: Black Elk's Account of the Seven Rites of the Oglala Sioux.* Norman: Univ. of Oklahoma Press.
Buechel, Eugene, S. J.
1970 *A Lakota-English Dictionary.* Ed. Paul Manhart, S.J. Pine Ridge, S.D.: Red Cloud Indian School.
Burnette, Robert
1974 *The Road to Wounded Knee.* New York: Bantam.
Catlin, George
1844 *Letters and Notes on Manners, Customs and Conditions of the North American Indian.* 2 vols. Rpt. New York: Dover, 1973.
Charles, Lucille Hoerr
1945 The Clown's Function. *Journal of American Folklore* 58:25–34.
Collier, Donald
1944 Conjuring Among the Kiowa. *Primitive Man* 17:45–49.
Collins, Dabney Otis
1969 A Happening at Oglala. *The American West* 6:15–19.
Cooper, John M.
1944 The Shaking Tent among Plains and Forest Algonquians. *Primitive Man* 17:60–84.
DeLand, C.E.
1904/1906 Aborigines of South Dakota. *South Dakota Historical Collections* 3:269–86.
Deloria, Ella
1929 The Sun Dance of the Oglala Sioux. *Journal of American Folklore* 42:354–413.
1932 Dakota Texts. *American Ethnological Society Publications* 14:1–279.
*1937a MS. Dakota commentary on the Walker texts. *Library of the American Philosophical Society* 30(X8a.50):27–47
*1937b MS. Teton Sioux Folklore and Ethnology. Translations of the 259 Bushotter texts in the national Anthropological Archives. Smithsonian Institution, Washington, D.C. *Library of the American Philosophical Society* 30(X8c.3)

*1938 MS. Story of the Woman from the Sky. pp. 20–24 in Dakota texts from the Sword manuscript. Library of the American Philosophical Society 30(X8a.18)

Deloria, Vine, Sr.

1987 The Establishment of Christianity among the Sioux. In *Sioux Indian Religion: Tradition and Innovation,* ed. Raymond J. DeMallie and Douglas R. Parks, 91–112. Norman: Univ. of Oklahoma Press.

Deloria, Vine, Jr.

1973 *God is Red.* New York: Grosset and Dunlap.

DeMallie, Raymond J., ed.

1984 *The Sixth Grandfather: Black Elk's Teachings Given to John G. Neihardt.* Lincoln: Univ. of Nebraska Press.

DeMallie, Raymond J., and Robert H. Lavenda

1977 Wakan: Plains Siouan Concepts of Power. In *Anthropology of Power,* ed. Raymond Fogelson and R. Adams, 153–65. New York: Academic Press.

Densmore, Frances

1913 *Chippewa Music II. Bureau of American Ethnology Bulletin* 53.

1918 *Teton Sioux Music. Bureau of American Ethnology Bulletin* 61.

1931 "Lakota Fieldnotes." Manuscript, personal files of Omer Stewart.

1953 The Belief of the Indian in a Connection between Song and the Supernatural. *Bureau of American Ethnology Bulletin* 151:217–23.

Dorsey, George

1906 Legend of the Teton Sioux Medicine Pipe. *Journal of American Folklore* 19:326–29.

Dorsey, James Owen

1889a Teton Folk Lore. *American Anthropologist* 2:143–58.

1889b Teton Folk Lore Notes. *Journal of American Folklore* 2:133–39.

1894 A Study of Siouan Cults. *11th Annual Report of the Bureau of American Ethnology:* 351–544.

1897 Siouan Sociology. *15th Annual Report of the Bureau of American Ethnology:* 205–44.

Dozier, Edward P.

1962 Differing Reactions to Religious Contacts among North American Indian Societies. *Proceedings of the* 34th International Congress of Americanists. Vienna (1960): 161–171

*The reference notations are from John Freeman, *A Guide to Manuscripts Relating to the American Indian in the Library of the American Philosophical Society* Philadelphia: American Philosophical Society, 1966.

Driver, Harold E., and William C. Massey
1957 Comparative Studies of North American Indians. *Transactions of the American Philosophical Society* 47, pt. 2

Dudley, Guilford, III
1977 *Religion on Trial: Mircea Eliade and His Critics.* Philadelphia: Temple Univ. Press.

Duratschek, M. Claudia, O.S.B.
1943 The Beginnings of Catholicism in South Dakota. Ph.D diss., Catholic University of America, Washington, D.C.
1947 *Crusading Along the Sioux Trails.* Yankton, S.D.: Grail Publications.

Dusenberry, Verne
1962 The Montana Cree: A Study in Religious Persistence. Stockholm Studies in Comparative Religion, no. 3

Eliade, Mircea
1958 *Patterns in Comparative Religion* New York: Sheed and Ward.
1959 Methodological Remarks on the Study of Religious Symbolism. In *History of Religions: Essays in Methodology,* ed. Mircea Eliade and Joseph Kitagawa, 86–107. Chicago: Univ. of Chicago Press.
1964 *Shamanism: Archaic Techniques of Ecstasy.* New York: Pantheon.
1973 *Australian Religions: An Introduction.* Ithaca, N.Y.: Cornell Univ. Press.

Erdoes, Richard
1972 *The Sun Dance People.* New York: Random House.

Erikson, Erik
1945 Childhood and Tradition in Two American Indian Tribes. *The Psychoanalytic Study of the Child* 1:319–50. Rev. in *Personality in Nature, Society and Culture,* ed. C. Kluckhohn and H. Murray, 176–203. New York.
1946 Ego Development and Historical Change: Clinical Notes. *The Psychoanalytic Study of the Child* 2:359–96.
1959 Identity and the Life Cycle. *Psychological Issues* 1, no. 1 Monograph 1
1963 Hunters Across the Prairie. In *Childhood and Society,* 114–65. 2nd ed. New York: Norton.

Feraca, Stephen
1961 The Yuwipi Cult of the Oglala and Sicangu Teton Sioux. *Plains Anthropologist* 6:155–63.
1963 Wankinyan: Contemporary Teton Dakota Religion. Studies in Plains Anthropology and History, no. 2. Browning, Mont: Museum of the Plains Indians.

Feraca, Stephen, and James H. Howard
1963 The Identity and Demography of the Dakota or Sioux Tribe. *Plains Anthropologist* 8:80–84.

Fletcher, Alice
1882 The Sun Dance of the Sioux. *Proceedings of the American Association for the Advancement of Science* 31:580–84.
1883a The Elk Mystery or Festival. *Peabody Museum of American Archaeology and Ethnology Reports* 16/17:276–88.
1883b The Shadow or Ghost Lodge. *Peabody Museum of American Archaeology and Ethnology Reports* 16/17:296–307.
1883c The White Buffalo Festival of the Uncpapas. *Peabody Museum of American Archaeology and Ethnology Reports* 16/17:260–75.
1896 The Emblematic Use of the Tree in a Dakota Group. *Proceedings of the American Association for the Advancement of Science* 45: 191–209.

Forbes, Bruce David
1985 Rev. of Pipe, Bible and Peyote among the Oglala Lakota, by Paul B. Steinmetz, S.J. *The American Indian Quarterly* 9:84–87.

Forbes, William H.
1894 Traditions of the Sioux Indians. *Collections of the Minnesota Historical Society* 6:413–16.

Fowler, Loretta
1978 Wind River Reservation Political Process: An Analysis of Symbols of Consensus. *American Ethnologist* 5:748–69.

Fugle, Eugene
1966 The Nature and Function of the Lakota Night Cults. *University of South Dakota Museum News* 27, nos. 3 and 4.

Fürer-Haimendorf, Christoph von
1974 The Sense of Sin in Cross Cultural Perspective. *Man: Journal of the Royal Anthropological Institute* 9:539–56.

Gilmore, M. R.
1932 The Dakota Ceremony of Presenting a Pipe to Marshall Foch and Conferring a Name Upon Him. *Papers of the Michigan Academy of Science, Arts and Letters* 18:15–21.

Girardot, Norman J. and Mac Linscott Ricketts, eds.
1982 *Imagination and Meaning: The Scholarly and Literary Worlds of Mircea Eliade.* New York: Seabury.

Grobsmith, Elizabeth S.
1974 Wakinza: Uses of Yuwipi Medicine Power in Contemporary Teton Dakota Culture. *Plains Anthropologist* 19:129–33.

Haines, Francis

1938 The Northward Spread of Horses Among the Plains Indians. *American Anthropologist* 40:429–37.

Hallencreutz, Carl F.

1979 "Christ is the Mountain": Some observations on the Religious Functions of Symbols in the Encounter of Christianity and Other Religions. In *Religious Symbols and their functions,* ed. Harald Biezais, Stockholm: Almqvist and Wiksell.

Hallowell, A. Irving

1942 *The Role of Conjuring in Saulteaux Society.* Philadelphia Anthropological Society Publications 2.

1952 Ojibwa Personality and Acculturation. In *Selected Papers of the XXIXth International Congress of Americanists,* ed. Sol Tex, 105–12. Chicago: Univ. of Chicago Press.

1955 *Culture and Experience.* Philadelphia: Univ. of Pennsylvania Press.

Hassrick, Royal B.

1964 *The Sioux: Life and Custom of a Warrior Society.* Norman: Univ. of Oklahoma Press.

Hayden, F. V.

1863 Contributions to the Ethnography and Philology of the Indian Tribes of the Missouri Valley. *Transactions of the American Philosophical Society* 12:364–78.

Hertzberg, Hazel W.

1971 *The Search for an American Indian Identity: Modern Pan-Indian Movements.* Syracuse, N.Y.: Syracuse Univ. Press.

Hodge, Frederick W., ed.

1907/1910 Handbook of American Indians North of Mexico. *Bureau of American Ethnology Bulletin* 30.

Holler, Clyde

1984 Black Elk's Relationship to Christianity. *The American Indian Quarterly* 8:37–49.

Holy Rosary Mission

1963 *Red Cloud's Dream.* Pine Ridge, S.D.: Red Cloud Indian School.

Horton, Robin

1971 Ritual Man in Africa. In *Reader in Comparative Religion: An Anthropological Approach,* ed. William A. Lessa and Evon Z. Vogt. New York: Harper and Row.

Howard, James

1954 The Dakota Heyoka Cult. *Scientific Monthly 78:254–58.*

1955 Pan-Indian Culture of Oklahoma. *Scientific Monthly* 81:215–20.

1967 Half Moon Way: The Peyote Ritual of Chief White Bear. *University of South Dakota Museum News* 28, nos. 1 and 2.

1976 Yanktonai Ethnohistory and the John K. Bear Winter Count. *Plains Anthropologist Memoir* 11.

Hultkrantz, Åke

1953 *Conceptions of the Soul among North American Indians.* Ethnographical Museum of Sweden Monograph Series 1.

1956 Configurations of Religious Belief among the Wind River Shoshone. *Ethnos* 21:194–205.

1961 Owners of the Animals in the Religion of the North American Indians. In *The Supernatural Owners of Nature,* ed. Åke Hultkrantz, 53–64. Stockholm Studies in Comparative Religion 1.

1967 Spirit Lodge: A North American Shamanistic Seance. In *Studies in Shamanism,* ed. Carl-Martin Edsman, 32–68. Stockholm: Almqvist and Wiksell.

1969 Pagan and Christian Elements in the Religious Syncretism among the Shoshoni Indians of Wyoming. In *Syncretism* ed. Sven S. Hartman, 15–40. Stockholm: Almqvist and Wiksell.

1970 The Phenomenology of Religion: Aims and Methods. *Temenos* 6: 68–88.

1971 The Structure of Theistic Beliefs among North American Plains Indians. *Temenos* 7:66–74.

1972 An Ideological Dichotomy: Myths and Folk Beliefs among the Shoshone Indians of Wyoming. *History of Religions* 11:339–53.

1974 Conditions for the Spread of the Peyote Cult in North America. In *New Religions,* ed. Harold Biezais, 70–83. Stockholm: Almqvist and Wiksell.

n.d. The Development of the Plains Indian Sun Dance. In *Perennitas: Studi in Onore de Angelo Brelich,* 223–43. Rome: Edizioni dell' Ateneo.

Hurt, Wesley R.

1960a Factors in the Persistence of Peyote in the Northern Plains. *Plains Anthropologist* 5:16–27.

1960b A Yuwipi Ceremony at Pine Ridge. *Plains Anthropologist* 5:48–52.

Hurt, Wesley R., and James Howard

1952 A Dakota Conjuring Ceremony. *Southwestern Journal of Anthropology* 8:286–96.

Hyde, George

1937 *Red Cloud's Folk.* Norman: Univ. of Oklahoma Press.

1956 *A Sioux Chronicle.* Norman: Univ. of Oklahoma Press.

Jahner, Elaine
1987 Lakota Genesis: The Oral Tradition. In *Sioux Indian Religion: Tradition and Innovation,* ed. Raymond J. DeMallie and Douglas R. Parks, 45–65. Norman: Univ. of Oklahoma Press.

James, Bernard
1970 Continuity and Emergence in Indian Poverty Culture. *Current Anthropologist* 11:435–52.

Jorgensen, Joseph G.
1972 *The Sun Dance Religion: Power for the Powerless.* Chicago: Univ. of Chicago Press.

Jorgensen, Joseph G., and Richard Clemmer
1978 Rev. of *The Indian in America,* by Wilcomb E. Washburn. *The Indian Historian* 11:38–44.

Kaiser, Patricia L.
1984 The Lakota Sacred Pipe: Its Tribal Use and Religious Philosophy. *American Indian Culture and Research Journal* 8:1–26.

Kemnitzer, Luis S.
1970 Cultural Provenience of Objects Used in Yuwipi: A Modern Teton-Dakota Healing Ritual. *Ethnos* 35:40–75.
1976 Structure, Content and Cultural Meaning of Yuwipi: A Modern Lakota Healing Ritual. *American Anthropologist* 3:261–80.
n.d. Manuscript notes, personal files of Luis S. Kemnitzer.

Kroeber, Alfred
1933 Rev. of *Method and Theory of Ethnology,* by Paul Radin. *American Anthropologist* 35:765–66.
1948 *Anthropology.* New York: Harcourt, Brace.

LaBarre, Weston
1960 Twenty Years of Peyote Studies. *Current Anthropologist* 1:45–60.
1975 *The Peyote Cult.* 4th ed. New York: Schocken.

Lame Deer, John
1972 *Lame Deer, Seeker of Visions.* Ed. Richard Erdoes. New York: Simon and Schuster.

Laney, John
1972 The Peyote Movement: An Introduction. *Annual of Archetypal Psychology and Jungian Thought:* 110–31.

Lanternari, Vittorio
1965 *The Religions of the Oppressed: A Study of Modern Messianic Cults.* New York: New American Library.

Lewis, Thomas
1970 Notes on the Heyoka, the Teton Dakota "Contrary" Cult. Pine Ridge

Research Bulletin 11:7–19. Pine Ridge, S.D.: Public Health Service, Community Mental Health Program.
1972 The Oglala (Teton Dakota) Sun Dance: Vicissitudes of Its Structure and Function. *Plains Anthropologist* 17:44–49.

Linton, Ralph
1943 Nativistic Movements. *American Anthropologist* 45:230–40.

Lommel, Andreas
1967 *The World of the Early Hunters.* London: Evelyn, Adams and Mackay.
1970 Rev. of *Shamanism: The Beginning of Art. Current Anthropologist* 11:39–48. [Seventeen book reviews of Lommel's study, plus his précis and reply]

Lurie, Nancy Oestreich
1961 *Mountain Wolf Woman, Sister of Crashing Thunder: The Autobiography of a Winnebago Woman.* Ann Arbor: Univ. of Michigan Press.

Lynd, James
1862 The Religion of the Dakota. *Collections of the Minnesota Historical Society* 2:150–74.

McAllestar, David P.
1959 Peyote Music. *Viking Fund Publication in Anthropology,* no. 13.

McGee. W. J.
1897 The Siouan Indians: A Preliminary Sketch. *15th Annual Report of the Bureau of American Ethnology:* 153–204.

MacGregor, Gordon H.
1946 *Warriors without Weapons.* Chicago: Univ. of Chicago Press.

McLaughlin, Marie L.
1916 *Myths and Legends of the Sioux.* Bismark, N.D: Bismark Tribune Co.
1973 *Native American Tribalism: Indian Survivals and Renewals.* New York: Oxford Univ. Press.

Mails, Thomas E.
1978 *Sundancing at Rosebud and Pine Ridge.* Sioux Falls, S.D. Augustana College.
1979 *Fools Crow.* New York: Doubleday.

Malan, V. D., and Clinton Jesser, Jr.
1959 The Dakota Indian Religion: A Study of Conflict of Values. Bulletin 473, South Dakota Agricultural Experimental Station, Brookings, S.D.

Mallery, Garrick
1893 Picture-writing of the American Indians. *10th Annual Report of the Bureau of American Ethnology.*

Marett, R. R.

1934 Rev. of *The Method and Theory of Ethnology,* by Paul Radin. *American Anthropologist* 36:116–18.

Mekeel, Scudder

1943 A Short History of the Teton-Dakota. *North Dakota Historical Quarterly* 10:137–205.

n.d. MS. "Lakota Fieldnotes," manuscript, personal files of Scudder Mekeel.

Melody, Michael Edward

1978 Maka's Story: A Study of a Lakota Cosmogony. *Journal of American Folklore* 91:149–67.

Mooney, James

1892 A Kiowa Mescal Rattle. *American Anthropologist,* o.s. 5:64–65.

1896 The Ghost Dance Religion and the Sioux Outbreak. *14th Annual Report of the Bureau of American Ethnology,* pt. 2. Rpt. Chicago: University of Chicago Press, 1965.

1897 The Kiowa Peyote Rite. *Der Urquell,* n.s. 1:329–33. Leyden.

Neihardt, John G.

1961 *Black Elk Speaks: Being the Life Story of a Holy Man of the Oglala Sioux.* Lincoln: University of Nebraska Press.

Newcomb, W. W., Jr.

1956 The Culture and Acculturation of the Delaware Indians. Papers of the Museum of Anthropology, no. 10. University of Michigan.

Nurge, Ethel

1966 The Sioux Sun Dance in 1962. In *Proceedings of XXXVI International Congress of Americanists,* 102–14. Seville: Sevilla.

1970 *The Modern Sioux: Social Systems and Reservation Culture.* Lincoln: Univ. of Nebraska Press.

Olson, Paul A.

1982 *Black Elk Speaks* as Epic and Ritual Attempt to Revise History. In *Vision and Refuge: Essays on the Literature of the Great Plains, ed. Virginia Faulkner and Frederick C. Luebke,* 3–37 Lincoln: Univ. of Nebraska Press.

One Feather, Vivian, ed.

1974 *Ehanni Ohunkakan: Myths from the Walker Collection.* Spearfish, S.D.: Black Hills State College.

Oosterwal, Gottfried

1971 Comments (32–33), in Weston LaBarre, Materials for a History of Studies in Crisis Cults: A Bibliographical Essay, *Current Anthropology* 12: 3–44.

Opler, Morris E.

1936 The Influence of Aboriginal Pattern and White Contact on a Recently Introduced Ceremony, the Mescalero Peyote Rite. *Journal of American Folklore* 49:143–66.

Ortiz, Roxanne Dunbar

1977 *The Great Sioux Nation Sitting in Judgment on America.* Berkeley, Calif.: Moon Books.

Overholt, Thomas W.

1974 The Ghost Dance of 1890 and the nature of the Prophetic Process. *Ethnohistory* 21:37–63.

1978 Short Bull, Black Elk, Sword and the "Meaning" of the Ghost Dance. *Religion* [Lancaster, Eng.]:171–95.

Paige, Harry W.

1970 *Songs of the Teton Sioux.* Los Angeles: Westernlore.

Pettazzoni, Raffaele

1956 *The All Knowing God: Researches into early Religion and Culture.* London: Methuen.

Philip, Kenneth

1977 *John Collier's Crusade for Indian Reform 1920–1954.* Tuscon: Univ. of Arizona Press.

Pine Ridge Research Bulletin

1969 Public Health Services, Indian Health Service, Mental Health Program. Pine Ridge, S.D. No. 10.

Pond, Gideon

1889 Dakota Superstitions. *Collections of the Minnesota Historical Society:* 215–55.

Powers, William K.

1977 *Oglala Religion.* Lincoln: Univ. of Nebraska Press.

1982 *Yuwipi: Vision and Experience in Oglala Ritual.* Lincoln: Univ. of Nebraska Press.

1986 *Sacred Language: The Nature of Supernatural Discourse in Lakota.* Norman: Univ. of Oklahoma Press.

1987 *Beyond the Vision: Essays on American Indian Culture.* Norman: Univ. of Oklahoma Press.

Radin, Paul

1923 The Winnebago Tribe. *37th Annual Report of the Bureau of American Ethnology.* Rpt. Lincoln: Univ. of Nebraska Press, 1973.

1924 *Monotheism Among Primitive Peoples* London: G. Allen and Unwin. Rpt. as *Special Publication of Bollingen Foundation* no. 4, Basel: Ethnographical Museum, 1954.

1933 *The Method and Theory of Ethnology.* New York: McGraw-Hill.

Ray, Verne

1941 Historical Backgrounds of the Conjuring Complex in the Plateau and the Plains. In *Language, Culture and Personality: Essays in Honor of Edward Sapir*, ed. Leslie Spier, 204–16. Menasha, Wis.: American Anthropological Association.

Reigert, Wilbur
1975 *Quest for the Pipe of the Sioux: As Viewed from Wounded Knee.* Jean Fritze, Keystone Route 184, Rapid City, S.D.

Ricketts, Mac Linscott
1970 The Nature and Extent of Eliade's "Jungianism." *Union Seminary Quarterly Review* 25:211–34.

Riggs, Stephen
1869 *Tah-Koo Wakan: The Gospel among the Dakota.* Boston: Congregational Publishing Society.
1880 The Theogony of the Sioux. *American Antiquarian* 2:265–70.
1883 Mythology of the Dakota. *American Antiquarian* 5:147–49.
1893 *Dakota Grammar, Texts and Ethnography.* Department of the Interior, U.S. Geographical and Geological Survey of the Rocky Mountain Region. Rpt. Blue Cloud Abbey, Marvin, S.D. 1977.

Robinson, Doane
1904 A History of the Dakota or Sioux Indians *South Dakota Historical Collections* 2:1–523. Rpt. Ross and Haines, Minneapolis, 1967.

Ruby, Robert H.
1955 *The Oglala Sioux.* New York: Vantage.
1966 Yuwipi, Ancient Rite of the Sioux. *Magazine of Western History* 16:74–79.

Saler, Benson
1977 Supernatural as a Western Category. *Ethos* 5:31–53.

Saliba, John A.
1976 *"Homo Religious" in Mircea Eliade: An Anthropological Evaluation.* Leiden: E. J. Brill.

Sanford, Margaret
1971 Pan-Indianism, Acculturation and the American Ideal. *Plains Anthropologist* 16:222–27.

Schaeffer, Claude E.
1969 Blackfoot Shaking Tent. *Glenbow Alberta Institute Occasional Paper*, no. 5, Calgary, Alberta.

Schmidt, Wilhelm
1933 *High Gods in North America.* Oxford: Clarendon Press.
1935 *The Origin and Growth of Religion, Facts and Theories.* London: Methuen.

Schultes, Richard Evans
1938 The Appeal of Peyote (Lophophora Williamsis) as a Medicine. *American Anthropologist* 40:698–715.

Schwatka, Frederich
1890 The Sun Dance of the Sioux. *Century Magazine,* n.s. 17:753–59.
Shonle, Ruth
1925 Peyote, the Giver of Visions. *American Anthropologist* 27:53–75.
Sialm, Placidus, S.J.
1923 A Retreat to Catechists. *The Indian Sentinel* 3:78.
Silva, Antonio Barbosa da
1982 *The Phenomenology of Religion as a Philosophical Problem: An Analysis of the Theoretical Background of the Phenomenology of Religion, in General, and of Mircea Eliade's Phenomenological Approach in Particular.* Uppsala: CWK Gleerup.
Slotkin, J. S.
1952 Menomini Peyotism: A Study of Individual Variation in a Primary Group with Homogeneous Culture. *Transactions of the American Philosophical Society* 42, pt. 4.
1956 *The Peyote Religion: A Study in Indian-White Relations.* Glencoe, Ill.: Free Press.
Smith, John L.
1964 A Ceremony for the Preparation of the Offering Cloths for presentation to the Sacred Calf Pipe. *Plains Anthropologist* 9:190–96.
1967 A Short History of the Sacred Calf Pipe of the Teton Dakota. *University of South Dakota Museum News* 28:1–37.
1970 The Sacred Calf Pipe Bundle: Its Effect on the Present Teton Dakota. *Plains Anthropologist* 15:87–93.
Spider, Emerson
1987 The Native American Church of Jesus Christ. In *Sioux Indian Religion: Tradition and Innovation,* ed. Raymond J. DeMallie and Douglas R. Parks, 189–209. Norman: Univ. of Oklahoma Press.
Spier, Leslie
1921 The Sun Dance of the Plains Indians: Its Development and Diffusion. *Anthropological Papers of the American Museum of Natural History* 16:451–527.
Stanner, W. E. H.
1960 On Aboriginal Religion. *Oceania* 30:245–78. Rpt. in *Oceania Monograph,* no. 11 (1966): 25–58.
Steiner, Stan
1969 *The New Indian.* New York: Dell.
Steinmetz, Paul B., S.J.
1970 The Relationship Between Plains Indian Religion and Christianity: A Priest's Viewpoint. *Plains Anthropologist* 15:83–86.
1980 Pipe, Bible and Peyote Among the Oglala Lakota: A Study in Religious Identity. *Stockholm Studies in Comparative Religion* 19.

1984a *Meditations with Native Americans: Lakota Spirituality.* Santa Fe: Bear and Co.

1984b The Sacred Pipe in American Indian Religions. *American Indian Culture and Research Journal* 8:27–80.

Steltenkamp, Michael, S.J.

1982 *The Sacred Vision: Native American Religion and Its Practice Today.* New York: Paulist Press.

n.d. "The Catholic Life of Black Elk." Manuscript, personal files of Michael Steltenkamp, S.J.

Stewart, Omer

1944 Washo-Northern Paiute Peyotism: A Study in Acculturation. *University of California Publications in American Archaeology and Ethnology* 40:63–141.

1948 Ute Peyotism: A Study of a Cultural Complex. *University of Colorado Studies, series in Anthropology,* no. 1 Rpt. New York: Kraus, 1972..

1956 Three Gods for Joe. *Tomorrow: Quarterly Review of Psychical Research* 4:71–76.

1976 The Peyote Religion and the Ghost Dance. *The Indian Historian* 5:27–30.

1977 Rev. of *The Peyote,* by Weston LaBarre. *American Anthropologist* 79:930–31.

n.d. Manuscript notes, personal files of Omer Stewart.

Stolzman, William, S.J.

1986 *The Pipe and Christ: A Christian-Sioux Dialogue.* Chamberlain, S.D.: St. Joseph's Indian School.

Streng, Frederick J.

1980 Sacred or Holy, in *The New Encyclopaedia Britannica,* 15th ed. *Macropaedia* 16:122–26.

Tennelly, J. B.

1936 Letter to Adelbert Thunder Hawk, June 29, 1936. Marquette University Memorial Library. BCIM Box 235, Folder 12.

Thomas, Robert K.

1965 Pan-Indianism. *Midcontinent American Studies Journal* 6:75–83. Rpt. in *The Emergent Native Americans: A Reader in Culture Contact,* ed. Deward E. Walker, Jr., 739–46. Boston: Little Brown.

Thomas, Sidney J.

1941 A Sioux Medicine Bundle. *American Anthropologist* 43:605–9.

Turner, Harold

1980 New Tribal Religious Movements in *The New Encyclopaedia Britannica,* 15th ed. *Macropaedia* 18:697–705.

Tylor, Edward B.
1871 *Primitive Culture.* 2 vols. London: J. Murray. Rpt. New York: Harper Torchbooks, 1958.

U.S. Government
1883a Teller to the Commissioner of Indian Affairs, Dec. 2, 1882, in *Report of the Secretary of the Interior* in serial 2190, pp. xi–xii.
1883b Rules for the Courts of Indian Offenses, April 10, 1883. *Annual Report of the Commissioner of Indian Affairs.*
1916 U.S.A. v. Harry Black Bear. U.S. District Court for the District of South Dakota, Western Division No. 820, Sept. 7–8, 1916. Federal Records Center, General Service Administration, Kansas City, Mo.
1934a John Collier, Circular No. 2970 on Indian Religious Freedom and Indian Culture, Jan. 3, 1934.
1934b Letter of Rev. Lawler to the Superintendent of the Pine Ridge Reservation in File, "Sioux Indians, Indian Religion." Federal Records Center, General Service Administration, Kansas City, Mo.
1936 Letter of Pine Ridge Superintendent W. O. Roberts to Fred Daiher, assistant to the Commissioner, Sept. 26, 1936, 37805 OS. Federal Records Center, General Service Administration, Kansas City, Mo.
1978 American Indian Religious Freedom. Hearings before the U.S. Senate, Select Committee on Indian Affairs, 95th Congress on S.J. Res. 102, Feb. 24 and 27. [This bill was passed by both Houses of Congress.]

Vecsey, Christopher
1987 Sun Dances, Corn Pollen and the Cross: Native American Catholics Today. *Commonweal* 114 (June 5) 345–51.

Voget, Fred W.
1956 The American Indian in Transition, *American Anthropologist* 58:249–63.

von Franz, Marie Louise
1980 *Projection and Re-Collection in Jungian Psychology: Reflections of the Soul.* LaSalle: Open Court Publishing Co.

Wake, C. S.
1905–06 Mythology of the Plains Indians. *American Antiquarian* 27:9–16; 73–80; 323–28; 28:205–12.

Walker, J. B.
1917 The Sun Dance and Other Ceremonies of the Oglala Division of the Teton-Dakota. *Anthropological Paper of the American Museum of Natural History* 16, pt 2.
1980 *Lakota Belief and Ritual.* Ed. Raymond J. DeMallie and Elaine A. Jahner. Lincoln: Univ. of Nebraska Press.

1982 *Lakota Society.* Ed. Raymond J. DeMallie. Lincoln: Univ. of Nebraska Press.

1983 *Lakota Myth.* Ed. Elaine A. Jahner. Lincoln: Univ. of Nebraska Press.

Wallace, Anthony F. C.

1956 Revitalization Movements. *American Anthropologist* 58:264–81.

Wallis, Ruth A., and Wilson D. Wallis

1953 The Sins of the Fathers; Concept of Disease Among the Canadian Dakota. *Southwestern Journal of Anthropology* 9:431–35.

Washburn, Wilcomb

1975 *The Indian in America.* New York: Harper and Row.

Webb, H. G.

1894 MS. *The Dakota Sun Dance of 1883*, MS. no. 1394a, National Anthropological Archives, Smithsonian Institution, Washington, D.C.

Wissler, Clark

1905 Whirlwind and the Elk in the Mythology of the Dakotas. *Journal of American Folklore* 18:267–68.

1907 Some Dakota. *Journal of American Folklore* 20:121–31.

1912 Societies and Ceremonial Associations in the Oglala Division of the Teton-Dakota. *Anthropological Papers of the American Museum of Natural History* 11:1–97.

1926 *The Relation of Nature to Man in Aboriginal America.* New York: Oxford Univ. Press.

Yarrow, H. C.

1882 Some Superstitions of Live Indians. *American Antiquarian* 4:136–44.

INDEX

Aberle, David F., 98
Adams, Al, 28
Allen, Douglas, 4
Allen (Pine Ridge Reservation), 22–23, 25, 26, 32–35, 87–89, 90, 93, 94
Altizer, Thomas, 4
American Horse, Ben, 29
American Horse, Charles, 100, 107, 114
American Horse, Joseph, 107, 114–15, 124
American Horse, Leo, 18–19, 23
American Indian Movement, 6, 16, 32 37, 166, 167–68; Oglala Lakota identity, place in, 172–74
Around Him, John, 33
Ashly, Fred, 21, 25 154
Ate Ptecela; *see* Lindebner, Fr.
Attacks Him, Cordelia, 79
Author's Involvement, 35–39

Back, Sam, 28
Bad Warrior, Martha, 209
Barragan, Dr. Don Luis, 193
Bear Butte (Black Hills), 22
Bear Shields, Kermat, 79
Bearskin, John, 87
Beckwith, Martha Warren, 53
Beckwith, P., 209
Benedict, Ruth F., 44, 58, 172
Bennett, J. W., 173
Big Crow, Susie, 91
Big Road, Mark, 26, 66
Black Bear (old man), 114
Black Bear, Harry, 89
Black Bear, Jacob, 89
Black Bear, Paul, Jr., 89
Black Bear, William, 90–91, 93, 123
Black Bull, James, 22
Black Cat, John, 89
Black Coyote, 169
Black Crow, Selo, 23, 32–33, 34
Black Elk, Benjamin, 38, 191, 201–4
Black Elk, Nicholas, 38, 54, 56–57, 169, 176, 179–85, 200
Black Fox, 22
Black Horse, Charles, 28, 123
Black Whirlwind, 23, 26
Blish, Helen, 174
Blue Bird, James, 87, 88–89, 92, 93
Blue Legs, 26
Body of Christ: and the American Indian Movement, 154; Good Plume's interview, 154–56; healing in, 155; Oglala Lakota identity, place in, 174–76; and Peyote, 175; and the Pipe, 161; Row-

Body of Christ (*continued)*
land's interview, 153–54; Rowland's testimonial, 156–62; and the Sun Dance, 160; visions, 155–57; and yuwipi, 154, 160
Brennan, John R., 88, 90
Broken Leg, Philip, 91, 101
Broken Nose, Richard, 33
Brown, Joseph Epes, 11, 22, 38, 53, 54, 56, 58, 186–87
Buechel, Eugene, S.J., 18, 40, 46, 59, 99
Buffalo Calf Woman, 3, 53–57
Buffalo Gap (Pine Ridge Reservation), 46
Bull Bear, Leona, 50
Bullman, Tom, 93, 114
Burnette, Robert, 6, 209
Bushotter, 27, 166

Calf Pipe, history of, 15–16; mythology of, 53–57
Calico, (Pine Ridge Reservation), 25, 26, 33
Catches, Joseph, 91
Catches, Pete, Sr., 11, 22, 26, 32–35, 63, 91, 190, 191
Catches, Vincent, 91
Catholic Church on the Pine Ridge Reservation, 35–36
Catlin, George, 182
Charles, Lucille Hoerr, 82
Cherry Creek (Cheyenne River Reservation), 155–56
Cherry Seed, 22, 190
Chief, Douglas, 125, 128–29
Chips (old man), 19–20, 25, 26
Chips, Charles, 20–21, 25
Chips, Elllis, 20, 25
Chips, Godfrey, 20, 25
Collier, Donald, 19
Collier, John, 17, 91–92
Collins, Dabney Otis, 36
Cooper, John M., 19
Crazy Horse, 19–20
Cross, Dr., 90
Cross Fire; *see* Native American Church
Crow, Wilson, 195
Crow Dog, Leonard, 21
Custer, S.Dak., 149

Deadwood, S.Dak., 89
Definitions, 5–7
DeLand, C. E., 209
Deloria, Ella, 26, 27, 29, 40, 53, 55, 83
Deloria, Vine, Jr., 173–74
Deloria, Vine, Sr., 9
DeMallie, Raymond, 20, 40, 53, 54, 56, 180, 181, 186, 188, 200
Denby (Pine Ridge Reservation), 94, 103
Densmore, Frances, 17, 18, 26, 27, 42–43, 45, 49, 53–54, 56, 62, 65, 83, 87, 166, 187, 189, 200
Deon, Neulon, 125, 127, 128, 143
DeSersa, Esther, 38
Dorsey, George, 54
Dorsey, James, 2, 26, 27, 40–41, 55, 57, 166, 189
Dozier, Edward P., 163
Dream: of becoming a medicine man, 21; of a boy and a girl in the Sun Dance, 34; of being buried alive, 24; of Mesteth praying with the Pipe, 121–22; of misuse of Pipe and Peyote, 120–21
Dried Meat, 43
Driver, Harold E. and William C. Massey, 87, 89, 210
DuBray, 33, 79
Dudley, Guilford, III, 4

Duratschek, M. Claudia, O.S.B., 35–36

Eagle Bear, Phillip, 12, 96, 125–28, 137–38, 142–43
Eagle Elk, 20
Eagle Elk, George, 23, 46
Eagle Elk, Joe, 48–49
Eagle Feather, George; *see* Schweigman, George
Eagle Horse, 23, 26
Ecumenist I, 6, 37, 177, 187, 191–93; Oglala Lakota identity, place in, 191–93
Ecumenist II, 176–91, 192; Oglala Lakota identity, place in, 176–91
Eliade, Mircea, 4, 59, 177
Elk Boy, Ira, 12, 123–24
Enculturation, 174
Erikson, Erik, 5, 163, 189

Fast Horse, Pete, 190
Fast Wolf, John, 23, 26
Fast Wolf, Philip, 90
Federal legislation, history of, 16–17
Feraca, Stephen, 29, 63
Fire Thunder, 40
Fire Thunder, Reuben, 32–33, 34
Fletcher, Alice, 40, 49, 54
Fools Crow, Frank, 8, 11, 22, 25, 26, 28, 29, 31–33, 38, 44, 47, 77, 78, 185, 186, 188, 190, 191
Forbes, Bruce, 177
Forbes, William, 209
Fowler, Loretta, 25
Fugle, Eugene, 63
Funeral services: of Ben Black Elk, 38, 201–4; of George Plenty Wolf, 205–8; of Rex Long Visitor, 36
Fürer-Haimendorf, Christoph von, 210

Gap, Eva, 95, 123
Gap, George, 95, 96, 103, 167, 196
Ghost Dance, 167, 200
Ghost Dance Messiah as Christ, 180–82, 200
Girardot, Norman J. and Mac Linscott Ricketts, 4
Good Lance, Frank, 22, 26, 44
Good Plume, Garfield, 12, 21, 153, 154–56
Good Voice, William, 33
Good Voice Elk, William, 23
Grabbing Bear, Bernard, 28
Grass Creek (Pine Ridge Reservation), 23
Green Grass (Cheyenne River Reservation), 11, 15–16, 172
Grobsmith, Elizabeth S., 22

Haines, Francis, 3
Half Moon; *see* Native American Church
Hallencreutz, Carl F., 37
Hallowell, A. Irving, 19, 164, 176
Hanbleceya, (Pipe Fast) etymology of, 59–60
Hand Soldier, John, 90
Hard Heart, Charles, 22, 26
Hassrick, Royal B., 54, 56, 166
Hawkins, James, 95, 167, 196
Hayden, F. V., 209
Hensley, Albert, 88
Herman, Jake, 30
Hertzberg, Hazel W., 166
Heyoka (clown), 82
High Hawk, Aloysius, 94
High White Man, Grant, 90
Hodge, Frederick W., 3
Holler, Clyde, 186–88
Hollow Horn, 22, 26
Holy Bird, 23, 26

Holy Rosary Mission, 31–33, 36, 91, 178, 183, 184
Horse Shoe, Palmer, 20
Horton, Robin, 8
Howard, James, 27, 82, 99, 166, 168
Hultkrantz, Åke, 4, 19, 22, 27, 41, 46, 63
Hunter, Lawrence, 11, 20, 28, 44–45, 64–65, 66–67, 101, 103–10, 122–23
Hurt, Wesley and James Howard, 63
Hyde, George, 3, 35, 209

Ice, Bernard, 12, 50–51, 89, 94, 100, 101–4, 106–9, 111, 120–21, 123, 124
Identity, nature of, 164–70
Indian religious freedom, 16–17
Iron Bear, James, 93
Iron Rope, John, 11, 22, 26, 31, 36, 45, 47, 62, 63–64, 65, 190
Iron Shell, 56

Jahner, Elaine, 40, 53
James, Bernard, 164–65
Janis, Pat, 33
Johnson, Rev. A. F., 91
Jorgensen, Joseph G., 189
Jorgensen, Joseph G. and Richard Clemmer, 1, 31–32, 174, 189–90
Kaiser, Patricia L., 179
Keith, Sidney, 16
Kemnitzer, Luis S., 49, 66, 191, 210, 211
Kills Brave, Sam, 183
Kills Enemy, Nellie, 91
Kills Enemy, Noah, 28
Kills First, Jim, 109
Kills Ree, Charles, 22, 26, 190
King, Matthew, 79
Kroeber, Alfred, 7, 15, 172
Kyle (Pine Ridge Reservation), 22, 25, 26, 28, 33

LaBarre, Weston, 1, 87, 89, 99, 193
Lakota; *see* Oglala Lakota
Laney, John, 151
Lanternari, Vittorio, 87
Lawler, Rev., 28
Lee, J. M., Captain, 56
Lewis, Thomas, 29
Lindebner, Fr., 184
Linton, Ralph, 163, 174
Little Eagle, Shirley, 48–49
Little Stallion, 114
Little Warrior, 22, 26
Living Bear, 22, 26
Loafer Camp (Pine Ridge Reservation), 91
Lommel, Andreas, 19
Lone Bear, Sam, 91
Lone Goose, John, 183, 185
Lone Man, 55
Long Visitor, Rex, 31, 36
Looking Horse, Orval, 15
Looking Horse, Stanley, 15–16, 66, 84
Looks Twice, Lucy, 11, 39, 183–85
Lurie, Nancy, Oestreich, 88
Lynd, James, 40

McGee, W. J., 3, 15, 40, 169, 172
MacGregor, James, 5, 18, 92, 165
McLaughlin, Marie L., 53
Mails, Thomas, 11, 22, 25, 28, 29, 32, 57, 182–83, 185, 190, 209
Makes Shine, John, 43
Malan, V. D. and Clinton Jesser, Jr., 174
Mallery, Garrick, 15, 54, 56, 210
Manderson (Pine Ridge Reservation), 22, 25, 28, 38, 60, 89, 91, 183
Marett, R. R., 7
Marrow Bone, Ben, 91
Martin, Joseph, 91

Martin, S.Dak., 88, 112
Means, Russell, 168
Mekeel, Scudder, 54, 209
Melody, Michael Edward, 53
Mesteth, Francis, 103, 106, 121–22
Mesteth, Phyllis, 91
Method of interpreting the field material, 7–8, 10
Mexican, Charles, 26
Mills, Renee, 93, 195
Minneapolis-St. Paul, 6
minor ceremonies (traditional religion), 82–83
Monotheism, 39–43
Mooney, James, 54, 56, 167, 169, 193–94
Morgan, George, 92
Marrow Bone, Ben, 91
Moves Camp, Bernard, 19
Moves Camp, James, Sr., 20, 21, 25
Moves Camp, Richard, 11, 20, 21, 25, 33, 84, 158–59
Moves Camp, Sam, Jr., 20, 23, 26
Moves Camp, Sam, Sr., 20, 21, 25
Martin, Joseph, 91
Mountain Wolf Woman, 88

Native American Church
  baptism in, 93–94
  ceremonial objects, 101–7; altar, 101–3; cedar, 106–7; charters, 90; drum, 103–5; gourd rattle, 107; staff, 106
  Cross Fire fireplace, 88–91, 93–94, 98, 101, 103, 193–95, 112–20; Oglala Lakota identity, place in, 193–95
  Deadwood trial, 89–90
  God, belief in, 98
  Half Moon fireplace, 88–91, 93–94, 98, 101, 103, 109–12, 196–97; Oglala Lakota identity, place in, 196–97
  history of, 87–96
  healing in, 122–24
  lack of healing in, 124–25
  last days, 108–9
  meetings: Author's return from Scotland, 125–43; Fourth memorial meeting for young girl, 144–51; Jungian analysis of, 151
  morning water woman, 107–8
  mutual influence of Half Moon and Cross Fire, 93–94
  Papal Blessing, 97–98, 125, 130, 134, 138, 139, 143
  Peyote, etymology of, 99
  Pipe used in meeting, 89, 127, 128, 134, 135, 137–41
  South Dakota law prohibiting transportation of Peyote, 90
  visions, 109–20
Neihardt, John C., 11, 20, 38, 181, 183
Newcomb, W. W. Jr., 166
No Horse, Dawson, 11, 22, 26, 47–48, 65, 66, 78, 79
Norris, S.Dak., 21, 155
Nurge, Ethel, 29–31

Oglala (Pine Ridge Reservation), 23, 26, 28, 33
Oglala Lakota: definition of, 3; literature on, 209
Oglala Lakota identity
  and the American Indian Movement, 172–74
  and the Body of Christ Church, 174–76
  and the Ecumenist I group, 191–93

Oglala Lakota identity (*continued*)
and the Ecumenist II group, 176–91
and the Native American Church, Cross Fire, 193–95
and the Native American Church, Half Moon, 196–97
complexities: from within, 165–66; from without, 166–70
contemporary modifications, 164–65
full blood vs. mixed blood, 165–66
model of, 170–72
pan-Indian influences, 166–68
psychological persistence, 164
Oglala Lakota Religion, definition of, 5
Oglala Lakota Traditional Religion
Author's involvement in, 35–39; Ceremonies: minor ceremonies, 82; Offering the Pipe to The Four Directions, 57; The Pipe Fast, 59–63; The Sun Dance, 77–82; The Sweat Lodge, 58–59; The Yuwipi Ceremony, 63–77;
God, belief in, 39–43
healing, belief in, 47–49
life after death, belief in, 49–53
One Feather, Vivian, 53
Oosterwal, Gottfried, 9
Opler, Morris, 194
Ortiz, Roxanne Dunbar, 21, 173
Our Lady of the Sioux, Indian murals in, 36
Overholt, Thomas W., 176
Owners of the animals, 46–47
Paige, Harry W., 28, 36
Paul VI, Pope, 97, 98, 125, 130, 134, 137–39
Payabya (Pine Ridge Reservation), 183
Pettazzoni, Raffaele, 39, 40
Peyote: availability of, 92–93; diffusion on the Pine Ridge Reservation, 90–91; diffusion to the Pine Ridge Reservation, 89–90
Phenonmenology, 4
Philip, Kenneth, 90, 209
Phillips, Percy, 55
Pine Creek (Pine Ridge Reservation), 91
Pine Ridge, town of, 22, 32, 44, 51, 91, 93, 121, 124, 136
Pine Ridge Research Bulletin, 167
Pipe ceremony at the funeral of Rex Long Visitor, 36
Pipe Fast, 59–63
Pipe, Peyote and Papal Blessing in Native American Church meeting, 134, 137, 138–140
Plenty Wolf, George, 11, 22, 26, 30–31, 47, 56, 60, 61, 63, 84, 178–79, 190, 205–8
Plenty Wolf's yuwipi meeting, 68–77
Pond, Gideon, 40
Poor Bear, Enos, 38
Poor Thunder, George, 22, 26, 29
Porcupine (Pine Ridge Reservation), 25, 26, 28, 32–35, 77, 81, 90, 136, 144
Potato Creek (Pine Ridge Reservation), 90, 98, 136, 144
Powers, William K., 18, 19, 40, 49, 50, 58, 63, 66, 167, 168–69, 177–79, 189, 191, 192
Price, Hiram, 16
Primal Religion, 7
Purpose of Study, 1, 9

Qualifications of principal informants, 10–12

Radin, Paul, 7–8, 9–10, 40–41, 88
Rapid City, S.Dak., 107
Rave, John, 87
Ray, Verne, 19, 82
Real Bull, James, 89
Red Bear (old man), 88, 89, 94, 95, 123, 167, 196
Red Bear, Charles, 90
Red Bear, Solomon, Jr., 92, 124, 167, 196
Red Cloud, Bernard, 12, 19, 88, 89, 91, 94, 96, 99–100, 105–7, 124, 128, 138, 141, 144
Red Cloud, Charlotte, 126
Red Cloud, Chief, 27, 35, 157
Red Cloud, Christine, 94, 124
Red Cloud, Edgar, 11, 30, 31, 81–82, 190
Red Cloud, Marie, 33
Red Cloud Community, 11, 22, 25, 26, 57
Red Elk, Steve, 22, 91
Red Star, Mark, 22, 23, 26
Reigert, Wilbur, 16, 209
Rich, Eddie, 21, 153–56
Richards, Frances, 106, 150
Richards, Reno, 33
Richards, William, 106, 195
Ricketts, Mac Linscott, 4, 209
Riggs, Stephen, 27, 40
ritual violation, 83–85
Roberts, W. O., 92
Robinson, Doane, 3, 209
Rockyford (Pine Ridge Reservation), 91
Rosebud Reservation, 12, 21, 23, 27, 49, 90, 96, 114, 126, 127, 136
Rowland, Eugene, 12, 153–54, 156–62
Rowland, Pedro, 156
Ruby, Robert, 22
Running Bear, Albert, 90
Running Bear, Richard, 89, 90
Running Hawk, Joseph, 91
Running Hawk, William, 91

Sacred and profane, 59
Saler, Benson, 41
Saliba, John A., 4
Sanford, Margaret, 166
Schaeffer, Claude E., 19
Schmidt, Wilhelm, 39
Schwatka, Frederick, 209
Schweigman, George, 29, 30, 182
Scottsbluff, Nebr., 109, 136
Shonle, Ruth, 87, 89, 210
Sialm, Placidus, S.J., 188
Sierra, Joe, 91, 103, 109, 110–11, 127, 137
Silva, Antonio Barbosa da, 4
Sin: ancestral, 84–85; cross cultural study, 210
Sitting Hawk, Levi, 89, 90
Slim Butte (Pine Ridge Reservation), 11, 22, 25, 36, 61, 91
Sloan, Thomas, 90
Slotkin, J. S., 87
Smith, John, 15, 16, 54, 55
Spider, Cynthia, 126
Spider, Emerson, 12, 88, 93–96, 105, 111, 112, 114, 123, 125, 127, 133, 137, 178, 193, 194–95
Spider, Jesse, 126
Spider-Mills, Verolo, 195
Spier, Leslie, 33
Spirits, belief in, 43–47
Spiritual food, 51–53
Spotted Crow, 28, 81
Spotted Eagle, Oscar, 123
Stanner, W. E. H., 9

Stead, Robert, 23, 45, 46
Steiner, Stan, 209
Steinmetz, Paul B., S.J., 31–32, 35–36, 53, 57, 125–43, 187, 188, 190, 211
Steltenkamp, Michael, S.J., 11, 22, 183–85
Stewart, Omer, 87–89, 91, 96, 167, 194
Stirrup, 22
Stolzman, William, S.J., 36–37, 210
Stoneman, Charles, 132
Streng, Frederick, 83, 210
Sweat lodge ceremony, 58–59
Swift Bird, Pete, 11, 23, 28
Sword, George, 41–42, 55
Sun Bear, Jesse, 90
Sun Dance: American Indian Movement presence in, 31–32, 34–35; author's participation in, 30–32; characteristics (recent), 32–35; ceremony described, 77–81; history of, 26–35; Mass celebrated with, 30–31; piercing of men, 29; piercing of women, 34; songs, 81–82
Swift Bird, Pete, 11, 23, 28

Taboo, 83–84
Teller, H. M., 16, 17
Tennelly, J. B., 92
Thomas, Robert K., 166
Thomas, Sidney J., 16, 209
Thunder Bear, 22
Thunder Hawk, Adelbert, 92
Thunder Hawk, Sarah, 33
Trimble, Al, 32
Turner, Harold, 7
Two Bulls, Matthew, 28, 191
Two Dogs, Ricky, 33
Two Eagle, Oscar, 123
Two Runs, Ernest, 55
Tylor, Edward, 39

Visions: Peyote 109–20; traditional Lakota, 48, 60–63
Voget, Fred W., 163
von Franz, Marie Louise, 4–5

Wake, C. S., 53
Wakpamni, 22, 48
Walker, J. B., 17, 26, 40–42, 53, 54, 56, 59, 182
Wallace, Anthony F. C., 163
Wallis, Ruth and Wilson D. Wallis, 85
Wanblee (Pine Ridge Reservation), 11, 20, 21, 25, 32, 33
Washburn, Wilcomb, 32
Washington, D.C., 16, 29, 35, 92
Weasel, 23
Weasel Bear, Beatrice, 12, 91, 96, 100, 103, 106, 110, 123–26, 137
Weasel Bear, Cleo, 142
Weasel Bear, John, 12, 96, 106, 109, 126, 129–33, 196–97
Webb, H. G., 209
Werner, Hon. Theo B., 92
White, Frank, 90
White Bear, Phillip, 91
White Bull, 112–14
White Calf, Richard, 28
White Clay, Nebr., 28
White Face, Matthew, 123
White Plume, 23, 26
Wilson, Dick, 32
Wissler, Clark, 38, 53, 82, 87, 172, 174
Wolf Creek (Pine Ridge Reservation), 23, 25, 28, 33, 91, 155, 156
Wounded, Charles, 91

Wounded Knee (Pine Ridge Reservation), 23, 25, 26, 89, 91, 93, 136, 167, 168, 173

Yarrow, H. C., 209
Yellow Boy, 78
Yellow Boy, Charles, 88
Yellow Boy, Silas, 88, 89, 127
Yuwipi ceremonies: changes in, 65; Chips family chart, 20; darkness, 64–65; disapproval of, 24–25; etymology of, 18; healing in, 47–49; history of, 18–26; Plenty Wolf's ceremony, 68–77; revival of, 18–19; songs, 65–67; Sun Dance song used in, 65–66; table of yuwipi men, 25–26; vision of devil and helpers, 24; young men's inability to handle power, 25